THE IX AGE
FANTASY BATTLES

Rulebook

2nd Edition, version 2.0

December 21, 2018

Written *by* the T9A Team

Published *by* Kevin Krüger, Burgstraße 31, 67105 Schifferstadt, Germany

Printed *by* Amazon Media EU S.à r.l., 5 Rue Plaetis, L-2338, Luxembourg

ISBN: 9781792189159

Contents

1 Introduction

1.A What is The 9ᵗʰ Age: Fantasy Battles?

The 9th Age: Fantasy Battles, often simply called The 9th Age or T9A, is a community-made miniatures wargame in which two grand armies clash in an epic battle for power or survival. Each army can be composed of simple foot soldiers, skilled archers, armour-clad knights, powerful wizards, legendary heroes, epic monsters, and huge dragons. The game is usually played on a 72″ by 48″ battlefield and uses six-sided dice to resolve different actions such as charging into battle, letting arrows loose, or casting spells.

All relevant rules, as well as feedback and suggestions, can be found and given here:

https://www.the-ninth-age.com/

All changes can be found in the change log:

https://www.the-ninth-age.com/archive.html

- Keywords and titles main terms are indicated by using capitalisation, as in "Round of Combat", unless they are too common, like "model" or "unit".

- **Bold font** is used to highlight essential words and Model Rules given by another Model Rule. It is used in Army Books to highlight Model Rules that are defined in the unit entry.

- *Italic font* is used for spell names, background text, or repetitive text.

- Grey-coloured text is used for figure and table captions, item restrictions, and repetitive text.

- (Brackets) are used for clarifications and explanations of the actual rules, and for defining parameters of some Model Rules.

The electronic version of this document has clickable hyperlinks colour-coded like this sentence, and the page footer displays hyperlinks to key sections.

Edited with LaTeX.

1.B Scale of the Game

Playing tabletop wargames is often an exercise in abstract thought, especially when it comes to mass battle games like The 9ᵗʰ Age. As such there is no prescribed scale while playing The 9ᵗʰ Age; a single miniature could represent a single, a dozen, or even a hundred warriors. We believe the timescale of the game to be even more arbitrary than the scale of the game: The action of moving in the Movement Phase could take several minutes of real time, while casting spells in the Magic Phase or shooting a weapon in the Shooting Phase could be near instantaneous events. Likewise the actions of two units clashing in the Melee Phase could represent only a few heartbeats in real time, while a Duel between two mighty individuals could be a drawn combat lasting several minutes or more. Hence, no quantitative value can be assigned to a game turn or turn sub-phase.

2   General Principles

2.A   Turns

The 9th Age: Fantasy Battles is a turn based game. A standard game lasts for 6 Game Turns, each divided into two Player Turns. At the beginning of the game, one player has the first Player Turn, in which they use their units to perform various actions, such as moving, casting spells, or Charging, while their opponent gets to react. After this, the other player has their first Player Turn. When this comes to an end, Game Turn 1 is complete. In Game Turn 2, the first player now has their second Player Turn, and so on, until both players have completed 6 Player Turns. This marks the end of the game.

2.A.a   Player Turn

Each Player Turn is divided into five phases, performed in the following order:

1	Charge Phase
2	Movement Phase
3	Magic Phase
4	Shooting Phase
5	Melee Phase

2.A.b   Active and Reactive Player

The Active Player is the player whose Player Turn it currently is.

The Reactive Player is the player whose Player Turn it currently is not.

2.A.c   Simultaneous Effects

Whenever two or more effects occur at the same time, resolve effects controlled by the Active Player first. If there is a choice involved (such as abilities that may or may not be activated), the Active Player must declare the use of their abilities before the Reactive Player. Each player is free to decide in which order they resolve their own simultaneous abilities. Once both players have declared the use and order of their abilities, resolve their effects, starting with those of the Active Player.

- During the Pre-Game Sequence, consider the player that chose their Deployment Zone to be the Active Player.
- During the Deployment Phase, consider the player that finished deploying first to be the Active Player.

For example, if both players have abilities that may be activated at the beginning of the Magic Phase, the player whose Magic Phase it is must choose first whether or not they are using their abilities and in which order. Then the Reactive Player may choose to use their abilities or not. After that, the effects of the abilities from both sides are resolved, starting with the Active Player's abilities.

2.A.d   The terms Friendly and Enemy

The rules often refer to a friendly or enemy Player Turn, friendly or enemy models, friendly or enemy units, etc. In this context, the term "enemy" refers to your opponent's Player Turns, models, units, etc., while "friendly" refers to yours.

2.B   Dice

2.B.a   Rolling Dice

In The 9th Age: Fantasy Battles, dice are often used to determine random outcomes. The most commonly used type is the six-sided dice, referred to as a D6, with a range from 1 to 6. The effects of a dice roll are often dependent on whether the rolled value is equal to or higher than a set value (such as a dice roll that is successful if the dice rolls '3' or higher). This is often referred to as a 3+ (or 2+, 4+, 6+, etc.).

Multiple Dice: Sometimes you need to roll more than one of these dice at the same time. This is represented by a number before the type of dice rolled, such as 3D6, which means to roll 3 six-sided dice and add the results together.

Modified Dice Rolls: On other occasions, a dice roll may be modified by adding or subtracting a number, such as D6+1. In such cases, simply add the relevant number to, or subtract it from, the result of the roll.

Natural Roll: A natural roll on a D6 refers to the value of the dice, before any modifiers are applied.

Rerolling Dice: Lastly, some effects in the game call for rerolling certain dice, such as "failed to-wound rolls", or "Aegis Save results of '1'". When you encounter such situations, reroll the relevant dice. **Dice can only be rerolled once.** The second result is final, no matter the cause, source, or result, and the initial result is ignored for all rules purposes, unless specifically stated otherwise. Note that rerolling a dice is not considered a modifier.

2.B.a.1 Rolling a D3

The game sometimes requires the roll of a D3. This is performed by rolling a D6 and then halving the result, rounding up, so that the result can only be 1, 2, or 3. If the game requires a natural '1' or a natural '6' when rolling a D3, it always refers to the value of the D6 before halving.

2.B.a.2 Maximised Roll and Minimised Roll

For dice rolls subject to Maximised Roll, roll one additional D6 and discard the lowest D6 rolled. For dice rolls subject to Minimised Roll, roll one additional D6 and discard the highest D6 rolled. **These rules are cumulative** (e.g. for a roll affected by two instances of Maximised Roll, you roll two additional D6 and discard the two lowest D6 rolled). The results of the discarded D6 are ignored for all intents and purposes.

2.B.b   The Direction Dice and Random Directions

The Direction Dice is a special six-sided dice with all sides marked with an arrow. Certain rules may ask the player to determine a random direction. In such cases, roll the Direction Dice and then use the direction in which the arrow points.

Representing the Direction Dice with a Standard D6

Alternatively the Direction Dice can be represented by rolling a standard six-sided dice and using the side with a single dot (i.e. the '1') to represent the direction of an arrow as depicted in figure 1. If rolling a result of '1' or '6' ('1' and '6' are on opposite faces on a standard dice), use the central dot in the '5' to represent the direction of the arrow instead.

Figure 1: Representing the Direction Dice with a standard D6.

3 Models and Units

3.A Models

Models in The 9th Age: Fantasy Battles represent epic warriors, ferocious monsters, and lethal spell casters. Every miniature that stands on the same base is considered the same model (e.g. a dragon and its rider or a cannon and its crewmen are considered a single model).

The scale of miniatures most commonly used for The 9th Age ranges from 1:70 to 1:50 when compared to real-life sized equivalents for human-sized creatures. Many units are commonly represented by miniatures with a scale in the range of 25 mm to 32 mm (a common form of measuring human miniature size is measuring the model's height to the eyes). Players are welcome to interpret the scale as they like, as the distances used in the rules do not seem realistic if the scale of 1:1 compared to the actual size of the miniatures is used for the game.

The 9th Age does not officially support any particular product line, and you are welcome to play with whatever scale and miniatures you and your opponent have agreed upon. However, it is very important to make sure you mount your models (regardless of scale or size) on the correct base size for the unit entry.

Just as we can imagine that the combatants in the game are actually smaller than the miniatures that represent them, we can also imagine that a single miniature does not have to represent a single warrior. We could imagine a unit of 10 elite elven warriors representing exactly 10 elves or some other group size like 20, 50, or 100. At the same time a unit of 10 Goblin Raiders could just represent 10 goblins, but is more likely to represent some larger group of 100, 200, or 500.

Characters and monsters are meant to represent exceptional individuals and especially potent creatures that are worth entire regiments on their own. It may be easier to come to terms with a miniature of a character representing not just the character itself but also their bodyguards and assorted staff that might follow such a hero into battle.

3.A.a Bases

All models are placed on a rectangular or round base. Base sizes are given as two measurements in millimetres: front-width × side-length (e.g. most horse riders' bases are 25×50 mm). In some rare cases models have round bases. In these cases, only a single measurement is given: the diameter of the base (e.g. a common War Machine base is a round 60 mm base). For all rules purposes, only the base of a model is relevant and determines the model's location on the battlefield, while the miniature itself is not taken into consideration.

3.A.b Multipart Models

Models with more than one Offensive Profile are called Multipart Models (see "Characteristic Profiles", page 14). Each part of such a model has its own Offensive Profile and is referred to as a model part. For example, a cavalry model has two parts (the rider and its mount), while a normal foot soldier has a single part.

Sometimes a model has multiple identical parts. In this case, the name of the model part in the unit profile is followed by a number in brackets. For example, a chariot might have three charioteers, which would be noted as "Charioteer (3)".

Whenever a rule, ability, spell, and so on affects a model, all parts of the model are affected, unless the rule specifically states it only affects a specific model part. When attacking or shooting, each part of a Multipart Model uses its own Characteristics and weapons.

3.A.c Model Facings

A model has 4 Facings: Front, Rear, and two Flanks. The Facings are the edges of the model's base. Models on round bases only have a single Facing, which is considered to be their Front Facing.

3.A.d   Model Arcs

A model has 4 Arcs: Front, Rear, Left Flank, and Right Flank. Each Arc is determined by extending a straight line from the corners of the model's base, in a 135° angle from the model's Facings. Any object at least touching the line that separates two Arcs (even if only in a single point) is considered to be inside those Arcs. For rules purposes, models on round bases have a single 360° Arc all around, which is considered to be their Front Arc.

3.B   Units

All models are part of a unit. A unit is either a group of models deployed in a formation consisting of ranks (along the width of the unit) and files (along the length of the unit) or a single model operating on its own.

When forming a unit, all models in the unit must be perfectly aligned in base contact with each other and face the same direction. Models in a unit that are not in the first rank must be positioned so that another model is directly in front of them. All ranks must always have the same width, except the rear rank which can be shorter than the other ranks; this is called an incomplete rear rank. Note that it's perfectly fine for the rear rank to have gaps in it, as long as the models are aligned with those of the other ranks. Following these rules, you are free to field your units in whatever formation, as few or as many files wide as you wish, but this may affect rules that interact with the unit (see 3.B.b "Full Ranks" and 3.B.c "Close Formation & Line Formation" for examples).

Whenever a rule, ability, spell, and so on affects a unit, all models in the unit are affected.

3.B.a   Rank-and-File

Normal models in a unit are called Rank-and-File models (R&F). All models except Characters are R&F models.

3.B.b   Full Ranks

The Height of a unit determines how many models are needed in a rank in order to form a Full Rank (see "Model Classification", page 87). Units of Standard Height need 5 models, Large units need 3 models, and Gigantic units need 1 model.

3.B.c   Close Formation & Line Formation

Units are normally considered to be in Close Formation. Units in ranks of 8 or more models are instead considered to be in Line Formation. Units in Line Formation gain the **Fight in Extra Rank** Attack Attribute, but cannot add any Rank Bonus to their Combat Score (see "Melee Phase", page 66 for details on the formations' in-game effects).

3.B.d   Health Pools

All Health Points of a unit are part of one or more Health Pools. The Health Points of all non-Champion R&F models of a unit form a separate Health Pool, while the Champion and each Character joined to the unit each have their own Health Pool (see "Champion", page 104 and "Character", page 102).

3.B.e   Unit Boundary

A Unit Boundary is an imaginary rectangle around the outer edges of the unit. The Unit Boundary of units composed of models on round bases is identical to the area occupied by their bases (this means that their Unit Boundaries are not a rectangle but a circle). A unit usually cannot be inside another Unit Boundary, unless the units are overlapping (see figure 2 and "Interactions between Objects", page 10).

3.B.f   Centre of Unit

A unit's Centre is the centre of its Unit Boundary (see figure 2).

3.B.g   Unit Facings

A unit has 4 Facings: Front, Rear, and two Flanks. The Facings are the edges of the Unit Boundary (see figure 2). Units on round bases have a single Facing, which is considered to be their Front Facing.

3.B.h Unit Arcs

A unit has 4 Arcs: Front, Rear, Left Flank, and Right Flank. Each Arc is determined by extending a straight line from the corners of the Unit Boundary, in a 135° angle from the unit's Facings (see figure 2). Any object at least touching the line that separates two Arcs (even if only in a single point) is considered to be inside those Arcs. For rules purposes, units on round bases have a single 360° Arc all around, which is considered to be their Front Arc.

Many rules require the players to determine which Arc of a unit another object is Located in. Note that for rules purposes there is a difference between "being inside an Arc" as described above and "being Located in an Arc" (see figure 3):

- Models/units on **rectangular bases** are Located in the Arc which the centre of their Front Facing is in.
- Models/units on **round bases** are Located in the Arc which the centre of their base is in.
- Any **other** object is Located in the Arc which its centre is in.

If an object is Located **exactly** in two Arcs of a unit, it is considered to be Located in the unit's Flank Arc.

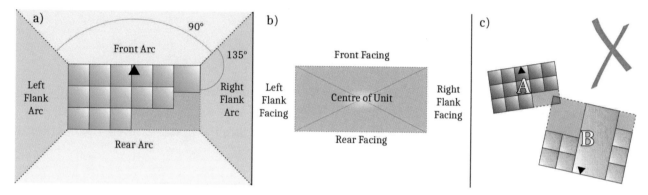

Figure 2: Unit Arcs, Unit Facings, and Unit Boundaries.

a) This unit has 3 ranks and 6 files. The base on the side is a Character with a Mismatching Base that has joined the unit (see "Mismatching Bases", page 96). The rear rank is incomplete and only contains 3 models.

The Front, Flank, and Rear Arcs are defined by drawing lines from the corners of the Unit Boundary in a 135° angle from the unit's Facings.

b) The Unit Boundary is the area drawn around the outer edges of the unit (grey area). The Centre of the unit is the centre of the Unit Boundary (red x).

c) A Unit Boundary cannot be inside another Unit Boundary, not even with parts that aren't occupied by any models.

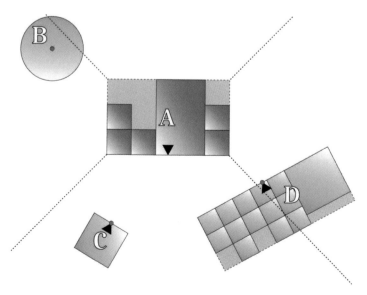

Figure 3: Units inside and Located in another unit's Arc.

Unit B is both inside unit A's Flank and Rear Arc. It is Located in unit A's Flank Arc (since this is where the centre of its round base is).

Unit C is inside unit A's Front Arc. It is also Located in unit A's Front Arc.

Unit D is both inside unit A's Front Arc and Flank Arc. It is Located in unit A's Flank Arc (since this is where the centre of its Front Facing is).

3.C   Interactions between Objects

There are many ways models, units, and other objects in the game interact with one another (see figure 4).

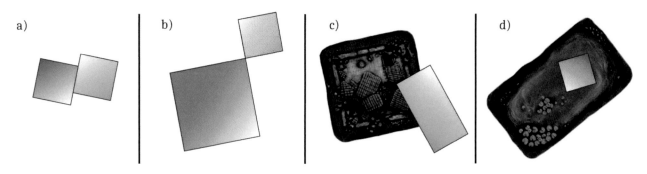

Figure 4: Interaction between objects.
a) Contact in a line   b) Contact in a single point   c) Partially inside   d) Fully inside

3.C.a   Base Contact between Units and Models

Two or more **units** are in base contact with each other if their Unit Boundaries are touching one another (including corner to corner contact).

Two or more **models** on rectangular bases are in base contact with each other if their bases are touching one another (including corner to corner contact).

3.C.a.1 Base Contact between Models across Gaps

Incomplete ranks or Characters with Mismatching Base may cause gaps between opposing models whose units are in base contact. Two opposing models are considered to be in base contact with each other across such gaps if you can draw a straight line from one model to the other, including corner to corner, that is perpendicular to the opposite Facings.

A model is considered to not be in base contact across a gap if its entire Facing opposite the enemy model is in contact with a friendly model.

See figure 5 for an example of how to determine if opposing models are considered to be in base contact across gaps.

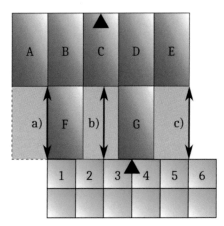

Figure 5: Base contact between models across gaps.

The unit at the bottom has Charged the unit on top in the Rear Facing. Due to the Charged unit's incomplete rear rank, some models are in base contact across gaps.

a) This line connects 1 with A and B. B's entire Rear Facing is however in contact with F, so 1 is in base contact across a gap only with A (it still is in "normal" base contact with F).

b) This line connects C with 2 and 3. C is in base contact with both 2 and 3.

c) This line connects E with 5 and 6. E is in base contact with both 5 and 6.

3.C.b Contact between Objects

Two objects, like bases, Unit Boundaries, Terrain Features, and so on, are considered to be in **contact** (see figure 4):

- If they touch one another:
    a) Along a line (e.g. two rectangular bases contacting each other along their front)
    b) At a single point (e.g. corner to corner contact between units)
- If one object is inside another. An object is considered to be **inside** another if it is:
    c) Partially inside the other object
    d) Fully inside the other object

3.C.c Overlapping Objects

Two objects are considered to be overlapping if they or their Unit Boundaries are at least partially on top of one another, without the two objects being in contact (e.g. a unit with Flying Movement and a Terrain Feature). This includes the edges of both objects.

3.C.d Interactions with Round Bases

Units are considered in base contact with a model on a round base if their Unit Boundaries are in contact.

Models are considered to be in base contact with a model on a round base if all of the following conditions are met:

- Their units are in base contact.
- The Unit Boundary of the model on a round base is directly in front of them.
- There aren't any models in between them.

See figure 6 for an example.

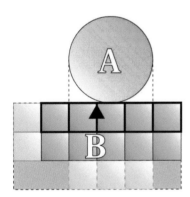

Figure 6: Base contact between models and a model on round base.

The models with a bold frame in unit B are considered to be in base contact with the model A on the round base, since this round base is directly in front of them.

4   Battlefield Logistics

4.A   Measuring Distances

The unit of measurement for all distances and ranges in The 9th Age: Fantasy Battles, is the inch ("). An inch corresponds to 2.54 cm.

When using 28 mm scale miniatures, 1" in the game would be roughly equal to 1.5 meters in real life. An average human-like creature in the game has an Advance Rate of 4" and a March Rate of 8", which means that in a single Movement Phase it would move only 6 metres (12 if marching). Likewise a ranged weapon like a Longbow has an effective range of 30" in the game which would equal roughly 45 metres, which is 5 times shorter than the average historic effective range of the weapon of around 250 metres.

For example, players could use the historic range of the Longbow to determine what kind of distance 1" represents in a game. In that case 1" would be slightly more than 8 metres and much closer to representing the distances assumed when writing the rules for this game.

We do not wish to tell players how to imagine their fights or how many individuals each miniature should represent, but we believe that an easy equation of 1" being roughly equal to 10 metres is a good representation of the size of the game. An average game will be played on a 72×48" table and thus represents a real-life area of 720×480 m or roughly 50 football pitches. In medieval times (the closest thing we have to our fantasy world) this would represent an average sized battlefield where two forces with soldiers numbering from a few hundred to several thousand would meet.

To determine the distance between two points on the Battlefield (or two units, or any other elements), you always measure from the closest points, even if the line of measuring goes through any kind of intervening or obstructing element.

The rules often refer to things being within a certain distance. Measure the distance between the closest points. If this distance is less than or equal to the given range, they are considered to be within range. This means that a model is always within range of itself, and that the entire model or unit does not need to be within range, only a fraction of it.

When measuring distances to and from a unit, measure to and from its Unit Boundary.

Players are allowed to measure any distance at any time.

4.B   Line of Sight

A model can draw Line of Sight to its target (a point, a model, or a Unit Boundary) if you can extend a straight line from its Front Facing directly to its target, without the line:

- Leaving the model's Front Arc
- Being interrupted by Opaque Terrain
- Being interrupted by the base of a model that has an **equal or bigger Height** than **both** the model and its target (see "Model Classification", page 87, for more details; Model Rules such as Tall or Skirmisher can affect this)

For the purpose of drawing Line of Sight to or from a point on the Battlefield, that point is considered to be of Standard Height.

When drawing Line of Sight from several models inside a unit, this is done independently for each model. Line of Sight cannot be drawn to targets outside the unit's Front Arc, and models never block Line of Sight to other models within the same unit. A unit is considered to have Line of Sight to a target if one or more models in the unit have Line of Sight. A model is considered to have Line of Sight to a unit if it can draw Line of Sight to any part of the unit's Unit Boundary.

See figure 7 for an illustration of how to draw Line of Sight from a model.

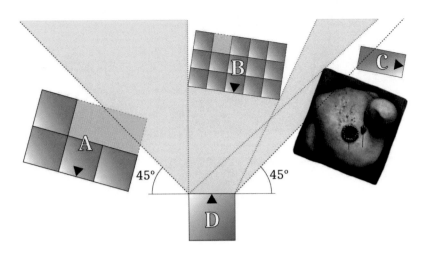

Figure 7: Drawing Line of Sight.

The area within which the single model unit D can draw Line of Sight is marked in yellow.

• Unit B is within Line of Sight.

• Unit A is within Line of Sight as unit D can draw Line of Sight to the Unit Boundary of unit A, even though that part of A's Unit Boundary is not occupied by any models.

• Unit C is not within Line of Sight as the Impassable Terrain Feature counts as Opaque Terrain and therefore blocks Line of Sight from unit D to unit C.

4.C   Unit Spacing

Under normal circumstances, all units must be separated from Impassable Terrain and from both friendly and enemy units by more than 1″ (remember that distances between units are measured to and from their Unit Boundaries).

Certain types of movement allow a unit to come within 1″ of other units or Impassable Terrain. The most common types of movement are:

- During an Advance Move, a March Move, or a Swift Reform, units may come up to 0.5″ of these elements but must be more than 1″ away at the end of the move (see figure 8).

- During a Failed Charge Move or a Charge Move, units are allowed to come within 0.5″ of these elements, including base contact (they may however only move into base contact with an enemy unit that was the target of the Charge).
  Once these units have moved within 1″ of these elements, they are allowed to remain there as long as they stay within 1″. As soon as they move farther away, the usual restrictions regarding Unit Spacing apply again.

See figure 8 for an example.

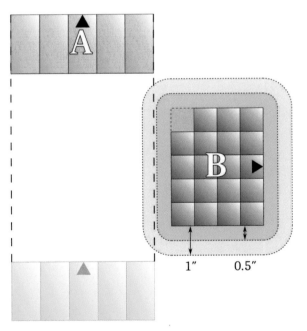

Figure 8: Unit Spacing.

During an Advance or March Move, unit A may be moved closer than 1″ to the Unit Boundary of unit B. Unit A may however not come within 0.5″ of unit B. Since unit A started the move more than 1″ away from unit B, it must be more than 1″ away from B's Unit Boundary at the end of its Advance or March Move.

5   Characteristics

5.A   Characteristic Profiles

Each unit entry contains the following Characteristic Profiles: Global Characteristics, Defensive Characteristics, and Offensive Characteristics.

5.A.a   Global Characteristics

Each model has three Global Characteristics:

Adv	Advance Rate	*The distance the model can Advance Move in*
Mar	March Rate	*inches. The distance the model can March Move in*
Dis	Discipline	*inches.*

5.A.b   Defensive Characteristics

Each model has four Defensive Characteristics:

HP	Health Points	*When the model loses this many Health Points, it is removed as a*
Def	Defensive Skill	*casualty.*
Res	Resilience	*How well the model avoids being hit in melee.*
Arm	Armour	*How easily the model withstands blows.*

5.A.c   Offensive Characteristics

If a model consists of more than one model part, each model part has its own set of Offensive Characteristics. Each model part has five Offensive Characteristics:

Agi	Agility	*Model parts with a higher Agility strike first in melee.*
Att	Attack Value	*The number of times the model part can strike in a Round of*
Off	Offensive Skill	*Combat.*
Str	Strength	*How good the model part is at scoring hits in*
AP	Armour Penetration	*melee. How easily the model can wound enemy*

5.B   Characteristic Values

Usually each Characteristic is rated with a value between 0 and 10. A higher value of a given Characteristic indicates that a model is more accomplished in that Characteristic. These values are used for various game mechanics like moving units and attacking with models, which will be explained in later chapters.

5.B.a   Random Characteristics

Some model parts have random values for one or more Characteristics (e.g. Attack Value D6+1). Roll for the value each time just before it is needed. In the case of Defensive and Offensive Characteristics, the rolled value is used for all simultaneous attacks (such as Shooting Attacks from a single unit or Melee Attacks at the same Initiative Step). When several models in the same unit have a random value for a Characteristic, roll separately for each model.

A random value for Advance Rate means that the model has the Random Movement Universal Rule (see "Random Movement (X)", page 97).

5.B.b   Special Cases of Characteristic Values

Sometimes Characteristic values in the Defensive or Global Characteristic Profile of mounts may contain a "C" instead of a value. In this case, "C" refers to the value in the Character's profile, which is used instead.

Sometimes a value is written as "C + X". In this case, use the Character's value, increased by X (see "Global and Defensive Characteristics", page 88).

In other cases, a model part may not have any values for certain Characteristics (e.g. the chassis of a chariot). These cannot be modified in any way.

5.C   Characteristic Tests

To perform a Characteristic Test, roll a D6. If the result is less than or equal to the value of the tested Characteristic, the test is passed. Otherwise the test is failed. A test always fails on the result of '6'.

When a model with more than one value for a Characteristic takes a Characteristic Test, take a single test for the Multipart Model, using the highest value available. For instance, if a Sylvan Elf Character with Strength 4 riding an Elven Horse with Strength 3 has to take a Strength test, the Multipart Model uses Strength 4 for this test.

When a unit as a whole takes a Characteristic Test, the highest value is used.

5.C.a Discipline Tests

Discipline Tests are a special type of Characteristic Test and follow their own rules. To perform a Discipline Test, roll 2D6 and compare the result with the model's Discipline Characteristic. If the result is less than or equal to the Discipline value, the test is passed. Otherwise, the test is failed.

When a unit as a whole takes a Discipline Test, the owner chooses a single model in the unit to take the test for the whole unit. If there are different Discipline values in the unit, the owner chooses which model to use. This often occurs when Characters are joined to units. If the model passes the Discipline Test, every model in the unit is considered to have passed the test. If the model fails the Discipline Test, every model in the unit is considered to have failed the Discipline Test.

Many different game mechanics call for a Discipline Test, such as performing a Panic Test or a Break Test. All these mechanics are Discipline Tests, regardless of any additional rules and modifications described in the relevant rules sections.

6 Modifiers

The values of Characteristics, dice rolls, or other values can be the target of modifiers from numerous sources, like spells, weapons, and armour. They can be set to a certain value, and they can be subject to addition, subtraction, multiplication, and division.

6.A Values Set to a Fixed Number

When a value or a roll is set to a certain value, replace the modified value or the required roll with that value. For example, if an attack is subject to the effect "The attack has its Armour Penetration **set** to 10", you replace the attack's Armour Penetration value with 10.

A Characteristic may be set to the value of another model's Characteristic. In this case, the value of the other model's Characteristic is taken after applying any modifiers which the other model is subject to. Modifiers that affect the recipient model will then be applied to this value (following the rules in Priority of Modifiers below). For example, if a model has the rule "The Discipline of all units within 12″ may be **set** to the Discipline value of the model", all units affected by this modifier may ignore their own Discipline and use the model's Discipline instead.

6.B Multiplication and Division

Sometimes values or rolls can be modified by multiplication or division. In case of the latter, round fractions up. For example, if a model attacks an enemy model that is subject to the rule "All attacks made against this model are performed at half Strength", the Strength of its attacks is divided by 2, rounding fractions up.

6.C Addition and Subtraction

Sometimes values or rolls are modified by addition or subtraction. For example, if a model is subject to the rule "The wearer gains +1 Armour and suffers −2 Offensive Skill", you add 1 to its Armour and subtract 2 from its Offensive Skill.

6.D   Priority of Modifiers

If any value or roll is affected by more than one modifier, these modifiers are applied in a strict order, following table 1 below. First apply modifiers listed with priority step 1, then apply modifiers with priority step 2 to the result, and so on (whenever you see the terms set/always/never used in bold in such a modifier, this indicates its priority).

When several modifiers within a group are to be applied to a value (e.g. a Characteristic value), apply them in the order that results in the lowest value.

When several modifiers within a group are to be applied to a dice roll (e.g. for Aegis Saves, to-hit rolls, to-wound rolls), apply them in the order that results in the lowest success chance of the roll.

Priority Step	Modifier
1	Values **set** to a certain number and values **set** to another model's value. If the other model's Characteristic is modified, apply these modifiers before setting the Characteristic.
2	Multiplication and division. Round fractions up.
3	Addition and subtraction.
4	Rolls **always** or **never** succeeding or failing on certain results, and Characteristics **always** or **never** set to a certain value or range of values.

Table 1: Priority of Modifiers.

For example, if a model is affected by (A) "The model's attacks gain +1 to hit" and (B) "Attacks made with this weapon are **set** to hit on 4+", first apply modifier (B), since modifiers using the "**set**" mechanic are applied in priority step 1, and then apply the +1 modifier, as modifiers using addition are applied in priority step 3. The final result would be the model's attacks hitting on 3+.

After all modifications via multiplication, division, addition, or subtraction, unless specifically stated otherwise:

- **Agility** and **Attack Value** cannot be modified to lower than 1.
- The value of all other Characteristics cannot be modified to lower than 0.
- **Armour** cannot be modified to exceed a maximum of 6.
- **Agility** and **Discipline** cannot be modified to exceed a maximum of 10.

7   Attacks

Units in opposing armies fight each other using melee weapons, ranged weapons, spells, and other unique attacks. This chapter will explain how attacks are performed in general and how you determine if they are successful in inflicting damage on their targets.

7.A   Classification of Attacks

All sources of damage are defined as attacks, which are then divided into Melee and Ranged Attacks (see figure 9).

7.A.a   Melee Attacks

All attacks made at units in base contact with the attacker's unit in the Melee Phase are **Melee Attacks**.

The most common type of Melee Attacks are **Close Combat Attacks**. Model parts perform a number of Close Combat Attacks equal to their Attack Value (see "Which Models can Attack", page 67).

Special Attacks are considered to be Melee Attacks that are not Close Combat Attacks (see "Special Attacks", page 114).

7.A.b   Ranged Attacks

All attacks that are not Melee Attacks are **Ranged Attacks**.

All Ranged Attacks made with a Shooting Weapon in the Shooting Phase or as a Stand and Shoot Charge Reaction are **Shooting Attacks**. Other Ranged Attacks include, amongst others, Damage spells, ranged Special Attacks, hits from Miscasts, and hits from failed Dangerous Terrain Tests.

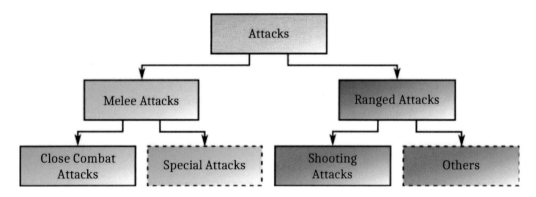

Figure 9: Classification of attacks.

7.A.c   Strength and Armour Penetration of Attacks

Attacks have a Strength and an Armour Penetration value, unless specifically stated otherwise:

- Close Combat Attacks use the Strength and Armour Penetration of the model part making the attack, possibly modified by their Close Combat Weapon, Model Rules, spells, Characteristic modifiers, and other effects.

- Shooting Attacks use the Strength and Armour Penetration in the profile of the Shooting Weapon they are made with.

- Other types of attacks (such as spells and Special Attacks) follow the general rules for their type and the individual rules specified in their description.

7.B   Attack Sequence

Whenever an attack is performed, use the following sequence:

1	Attacker allocates attacks if applicable.
2	Determine number of hits.
3	Attacker distributes hits if applicable.
4	Attacker rolls to wound; if successful, proceed.
5	Defender makes Armour Save rolls; if failed, proceed.
6	Defender makes Special Save rolls; if failed, proceed.
7	Defender removes Health Points and/or casualties.
8	Defender takes Panic Tests if necessary.

Complete each step for all the attacks that are happening simultaneously (such as all Shooting Attacks from a single unit or all Close Combat Attacks at a given Initiative Step) before moving on to the next step.

7.C   Allocating Close Combat Attacks

Close Combat Attacks are directed against enemy models in base contact. This is referred to as allocating attacks, and will be explained in the Melee Phase chapter (see "Allocating Attacks", page 68).

7.D   Determining the Number of Hits

Close Combat Attacks and most Shooting Attacks need to roll to hit (see "Rolling to Hit", page 69 and "Aim", page 62), while Special Attacks and certain spells may hit automatically, inflicting a fixed or random number of hits.

7.E   Distributing Hits

All attacks that target a unit as a whole will under normal circumstances hit the unit's R&F Health Pool. These include most Ranged Attacks and most Melee Attacks that are not Close Combat Attacks. How hits are distributed may change when Characters are joined to units, as described in "Character", page 102.

Close Combat Attacks are not distributed, but are allocated before to-hit rolls are made, as mentioned above. Do not redistribute the hits from Close Combat Attacks at this stage.

In cases where not all models of a Health Pool have the same relevant Characteristics or rules (such as different Resilience values or different saves), use the value or rules of the largest fraction of the Health Pool's models, and apply them to all rolls (to-hit, to-wound, saves). In case of a tie, the attacker chooses which fraction to use.

7.F   To-Wound Rolls

If an attack has a Strength value, it must wound the target to have a chance to harm it. To make a to-wound roll, roll a D6 for each hit. The difference between the Strength of the attack and the Resilience Characteristic of the defender determines the needed roll to wound the target (see table 2 below).

A natural roll of '6' will always succeed and a natural roll of '1' will always fail. The player whose attack inflicted the hit makes a to-wound roll for each attack that hit the target. A successful to-wound roll causes a wound; proceed to Armour Saves and Armour Modifiers.

If the attack does not have a Strength value, follow the rules given for that particular attack.

Strength minus Resilience	Needed roll to wound
2 or more	2+
1	3+
0	4+
−1	5+
−2 or less	6+

Table 2: To-Wound Table.

7.G   Armour Saves

If one or more wounds are inflicted, the player whose unit is being wounded now has a chance to save the wound(s) if the wounded models have any Armour. To make an Armour Save roll, roll a D6 for each wound. The following formula determines the needed roll to disregard the wound:

$$7 - (\text{Armour of the defender}) + (\text{Armour Penetration of the attack})$$

A natural roll of '1' will always fail.

If the Armour Save is passed the wound is disregarded.

See table 3 below for the different possible results of the formula.

Armour minus AP	Needed roll to disregard the wound
0 or less	No save possible
1	6+
2	5+
3	4+
4	3+
5 or 6	2+

Table 3: Armour Save Rolls.

7.H   Special Saves

The attacked model now has a final chance to disregard a wound that was not saved by its Armour Save, provided it has a Special Save. There are different types of Special Saves, like Aegis (X) and Fortitude (X), both detailed in "Model Rules", page 92.

To make a Special Save roll, roll a D6 for each wound that was not saved by the model's Armour Save.

- If X is given as a dice roll (e.g. Aegis (4+)), X is the roll needed to successfully disregard the wound.

- If X is given as a modifier and with a maximum value (e.g. Fortitude (+1, max 3+)), the model gains this as a modifier to all its Special Save rolls of the same type, which cannot be increased to rolls better than the maximum value given in brackets. If the model doesn't have that type of Special Save, it instead gains a corresponding Special Save ((7 − X)+) (e.g. a model with Aegis (+2, max 4+) will gain Aegis (5+)).

If a model has more than one Special Save, choose which one to use before rolling. Only a single Special Save can be used against each wound.

7.I   Losing Health Points

For each unsaved wound, the attacked model immediately loses a Health Point, which may lead to models being removed as casualties. See "Casualties", page 80 for further details.

Figure 10 summarises the steps from an attack to a potential casualty.

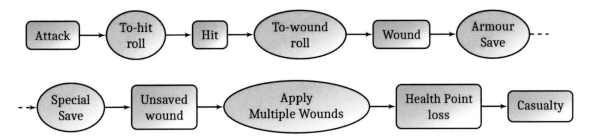

Figure 10: Flowchart of the steps from an attack to a potential casualty.

8 Setting up a Game

8.A Building an Army

The 9th Age: Fantasy Battles includes a series of Army Books which contain the unique rules for Characters and troops, and the descriptions of the different armies. All unit entries within an Army Book are divided into different Army Categories, which may be limited to represent a minimum or maximum percentage of the Army Points.

The first step in building an army is writing down a selection of units, options, and their Point Costs on a document called the Army List. An army is subject to certain rules and restrictions which this chapter will describe in further detail.

8.A.a Point Costs

Every unit, weapon, upgrade, Special Item, etc. costs a certain amount of points. The 9th Age uses Point Costs to balance units and options so two players can enjoy a game that tests their skills. This allows for quick pickup games between friends or helps design scenarios where you need to know how powerful certain things are. A unit's Point Cost is the total of its starting Point Cost and the Point Costs of all its upgrades. An army's Point Cost is the total of all its units' Point Costs.

8.B Army List Structure

Each army is divided into several Army Categories, restricting the selection of units in a way that enables players to enjoy a balanced and fair gaming experience. At the same time, they still ensure that armies used in the game can employ a wide variety of styles. This could represent a single Character and its hunting party or large armies numbering in their thousands clashing for the fate of the world.

All armies in The 9th Age: Fantasy Battles are subject to the basic composition rules detailed in this section.

8.B.a Army Points

Before building an army, you will want to decide with your opponent on the size of the battle, referred to as Army Points. The combined Point Costs of every unit in your army, as described in "Point Costs", page 22, **must not** exceed the Army Points. An army may fall below the limit by up to 40 points.

8.B.b Army Categories

An Army List is divided into Army Categories, and every unit on the Army List belongs to one or more Army Categories. These are marked by icons in the unit entries in the Army Book. The number of points a player can spend on each of these Army Categories is defined in each Army Book.

The Army Categories are divided into three groupings: the commanders and the outstanding individuals (Characters), the backbone of the force (Core and Special), and the thematic unique additions (Army-Specific). All armies **must** have units from the Characters and Core Army Categories in their Army List.

8.B.b.1 Characters

- This Army Category always has a maximum amount of points that can be spent on it, usually 40% of the Army Points.

- Each army must contain at least one Character that is eligible to be the army's General (see "The General", page 24).

- Unless specifically stated otherwise, entries that belong to this Army Category follow the rules for Characters given in "Character", page 102.

Characters represent the leaders and exceptional individuals who, through their particular sets of skills, influence the course of battle using either brute force, tactical acumen, spell casting ability, or engineering knowledge. It is they who muster the army, and your force will always include at least one representative of this Army Category to serve as your army

8.B.b.2 Core

- This Army Category always has a minimum amount of points that must be spent on it, usually 25% of the Army Points.

The Core represents the most readily available warriors a faction has access to and will form the bulk of combatants under the command of the Characters in the force. No matter where or why the faction fights, the Core are those units that will always be present in some combination as part of the fighting force. They are also those warriors that a society can provide for battle in the greatest numbers. While armies can overwhelmingly be formed out of the Core units, it is rarely the case as each commander seeks to deploy a force that contains as many of their finest or more specialised warriors as possible, depending on the

8.B.b.3 Special

- This Army Category has no maximum or minimum limit. You are free to spend any amount of points on units in this Army Category, so long as the requirements of the army composition are met.

The Special Army Category represents more specialised warriors. A faction can call upon large numbers of these warriors and they can often be the most numerous segment of the entire fighting force. However, their numbers are still limited, and though some of these units can form an entire battle line there just isn't enough of them to form armies on their

8.B.b.4 Army-Specific

- This Army Category has a maximum amount of points that can be spent on it; the limit is defined within individual Army Books.

- All armies have one or more Army-Specific Categories.

The Army-Specific Categories are introduced to provide additional limitations in the process of army building. These limitations are designed to be reflective of the nature of the faction in question, and with the goal of ensuring greater balance of the game. There are three types of Army-Specific Categories: one type is simply an additional grouping of units connected with a certain theme. These are given a thematic name reflective of the army they are part of or the function they perform (e.g. Orcs and Goblins – Death from Above). The second type of Army-Specific Categories provides limitations linked with a certain function a unit from another Army Category performs within the army (e.g. Beast Herds – Ambushers). And the third type of Army-Specific Categories is a mix of the above.

8.B.b.5 Units Belonging to more than one Army Category

Some units can be included in more than one Army Category, which is represented by more than one icon in their entry. In these cases, simply count the unit's Point Cost towards the limits of all its Army Categories, but only once towards the army Point Cost.

8.B.b.6 Adding Army Categories

Choosing certain options can make a unit count towards another Army Category in addition to its original Army Category. For example, giving a unit Shooting Weapons might make it also count towards the Ranged Support Army Category. This is marked by a small icon of the additional Army Category, displayed underneath the original Army Category icon(s), together with the conditions for counting in this additional Army Category.

8.B.b.7 Splitting Point Cost between Army Categories

In some rare cases a unit's Point Cost can be split between different Army Categories, where the Point Cost for some particular option is additionally counted towards a different Army Category than the unit. This is marked in the unit entry by a split icon, with the two halves representing the two Army Categories the unit counts towards.

For example, a 250 pts Elf Character, counted towards the Characters Army Category, decides to ride a 500 pts Dragon, which is an option marked to count additionally towards Beasts and Monsters. In this case, the player must count the entire unit's Point Cost (250 + 500 = 750 pts) towards Characters, and the Dragon's Point Cost (500 pts) towards Beasts and Monsters.

8.B.c   Duplication Limits and Restrictions

Certain units and options are limited in number in the army.

8.B.c.1 0–X Items per Army

Some items in the Army Books are marked with 0–X items per Army (e.g. 0–2 Units per Army, 0–2 Models per Army, 0–2 Mounts per Army). Such items can be included from zero to X times in the same army. The maximum limit (X) is halved for Warbands and doubled for Grand Armies, rounding fractions up (see below).

8.B.c.2 One of a Kind

Items (units, upgrades, equipment, etc.) marked as One of a Kind may only be taken once per army. This is not changed for Warbands or Grand Armies.

8.B.c.3 Minimum Army Size

Every army must contain a minimum of 4 units. Characters do not count towards this minimum. All units with the War Machine Universal Rule together count as a single unit for this purpose.

8.B.c.4 The General

A single Character in the army must be named the General. At least one Character must be included in the army that is eligible to fulfill this role. Who is the General must be noted on the Army List.

The General gains the Commanding Presence Universal Rule.

8.C Warbands and Grand Armies

The rules for army composition are modified depending on the size of an army. An army that is unusually small or unusually large is subject to the following rules.

<table>
<tr><td align="center">**Warbands**</td><td align="center">**Grand Armies**</td></tr>
<tr><td>Armies of 3000 points or less are called Warbands. The Minimum Army Size is decreased to 3 units.</td><td>Armies of 8000 points or more are called Grand Armies.</td></tr>
<tr><td>All "0–X Items per Army" limits are halved, rounding fractions up.</td><td>All "0–X Items per Army" limits are doubled.</td></tr>
<tr><td>The usual board size is 36″ wide and 48″ deep.</td><td>Adapt the board size to the size of the game.</td></tr>
</table>

8.D How to Read Unit Entries

Every unit in the game has a certain set of Characteristics and possibly optional or mandatory upgrades, and, as explained above, every unit is part of an Army Category. In addition, the models in that unit may be equipped with particular weapons and armour, and they may have one or more Model Rules, as you will learn in later chapters of this Rulebook (see "Model Rules", page 92).

Every unit is represented by its unit entry in its Army Book, and these unit entries contain all the information pertaining to that unit, including the data above as well as further information like Model Type and Height, base size, restrictions regarding the number of models or certain equipment, and so on.

This section will explain how the most common information in unit entries is presented in the Army Books of T9A.

8.D.a Common Unit Entries

Unit entries usually consist of a header, the unit profile, and options, as illustrated in figure 11.

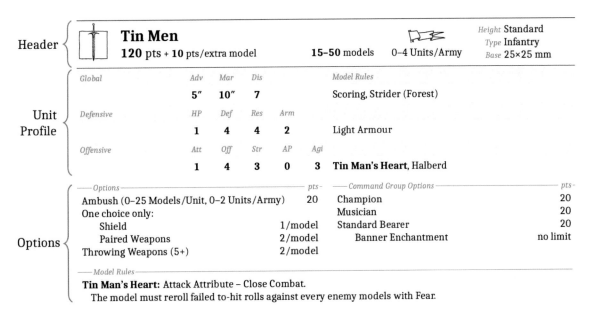

Figure 11: Common unit entry.

The header of a unit entry usually contains all the general information on the unit (see figure 12).

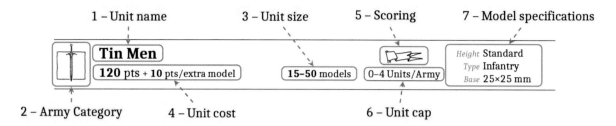

Figure 12: Header of a common unit entry.

1 – Unit name

This is the name of the unit that will be used e.g. when choosing the unit to perform an action like Charging, or when targeting the unit with a spell or a Shooting Attack.

2 – Army Category

Every unit is part of an Army Category, like Characters, Core, or Special, which is important e.g. for building an army or for certain Model Rules. Each Army Category is represented by an icon that corresponds to the respective Army Category as shown in each Army Book's section on Army Organisation.

Note that some units may belong to more than one Army Category (see "Army Categories", page 22). In this case the icons of all these Army Categories will be depicted.

3 – Unit size

The unit size tells you the minimum and the maximum size of the unit when building an army. The minimum unit size corresponds to the number of models that the unit must contain at least. And accordingly, the maximum unit size represents the number of models that the unit can consist of at the most.

In the example in figure 12, a unit of Tin Men must consist of at least 15 models when building the army, while you can add up to 35 models, attaining the unit's maximum size of 50 models.

4 – Unit cost

The unit cost tells you how many points you have to pay for adding the unit to your army in its minimum size, and how many points each additional model will cost. For some units in the game, an additional model will cost the same amount of points as a model that is part of the unit's minimum size, while for others additional models may be more or less expensive than the initial models.

In the example in figure 12, a unit of Tin Men consisting of the minimum size of 15 models will cost 120 points, while each additional Tin Man model will cost 10 points. So for instance a unit of 25 Tin Men will cost a total of 220 points (120 points for the first 15 models and 100 pts for the 10 additional models).

5 – Scoring

Some units have a certain Model Rule called Scoring, which is relevant for winning Secondary Objectives during the game (see "Scoring", page 98 and "Secondary Objectives", page 35). Units with this Model Rule will be marked with a pennant icon.

6 – Unit cap

Certain units can only be selected a limited number of times in an army. In this case you will find a "0–X Units/Army" cap in the unit entry. In the example, an army may contain up to two units Tin Men, regardless of their size, equipment, etc.

7 – Model specifications

Every model in the game has a specific Height, Type, and base size, which are relevant for a wide variety of game mechanics and Model Rules.

8.D.a.2 Unit Profile

The unit profile contains the models' Characteristic Profiles and Model Rules, including their mundane equipment (see figure 13).

	8 – Characteristic Profiles				9 – Model Rules	
Global	*Adv*	*Mar*	*Dis*		*Model Rules*	
	5″	10″	7		Scoring, Strider (Forest)	
Defensive	*HP*	*Def*	*Res*	*Arm*		
	1	4	4	2	Light Armour	
Offensive	*Att*	*Off*	*Str*	*AP*	*Agi*	
	1	4	3	0	3	**Tin Man's Heart**, Halberd

Figure 13: Unit profile of a common unit entry.

8 – Characteristic Profiles

The Characteristic Profiles of each unit entry contain the values of all of a unit's Global, Defensive, and Offensive Characteristics. Note that the values displayed here represent the models' unmodified Characteristic values, excluding any modifiers e.g. from Model Rules and equipment:

- For instance, in case of Armour, the Characteristic value displayed here represents the models' innate armour (granted e.g. from scales or a tough hide). Any armour from Armour Equipment, like Light Armour in the example above, will have to be added on top of the Armour value displayed in the Defensive Profile. In this example, the models will have an Armour of 3 (2 from the models' innate armour and 1 from their Light Armour), which will give them a 4+ Armour Save against attacks without any Armour Penetration (see "Armour Saves", page 20).
- The profile also displays the models' unmodified Strength and Armour Penetration. Any Strength and Armour Penetration modifiers, e.g. from weapons, will have to be added on top. In our example, the models' Close Combat Attacks will have a Strength value of 4 and an Armour Penetration value of 1, due to the innate Strength of 3 and the +1 Strength and Armour Penetration modifiers from the Halberds the models are equipped with.

9 – Model Rules

In this part of the unit entry, the unit's Model Rules are displayed:

- The Global Model Rules comprise the unit's Universal Rules (in alphabetical order).
- The Defensive Model Rules comprise the unit's Personal Protections and Armour Equipment. In case a unit has more than one Model Rule from these categories, Personal Protections will be listed first (in alphabetical order), followed by the unit's Armour Equipment (in alphabetical order).
- The Offensive Model Rules comprise the unit's Attack Attributes, Special Attacks, and weapons. In case a unit has more than one Model Rule from these categories, Attack Attributes and Special Attacks will be listed first (in alphabetical order), followed by the unit's weapons (in alphabetical order).

In some unit entries, you will notice certain Model Rules in bold, like Tin Man's Heart in the example above. Bold font is used here to highlight army-specific Model Rules that are defined in the unit entry.

8.D.a.3 Options

In this part of the unit profile illustrated in figure 14, you will find all the optional and mandatory upgrades that can be bought for a unit when building the army.

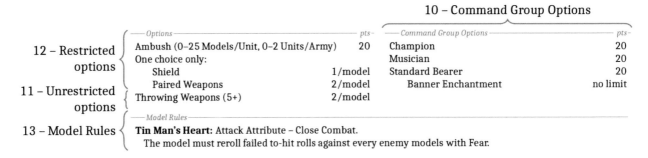

Figure 14: Options in a common unit entry.

10 – Command Group options

Certain units have one or more Command Group Options in their unit entry, which allow them to upgrade one model of the unit to a Champion, another model to a Musician, and another model to a Standard Bearer. This means that a single R&F model cannot be upgraded to be a Musician and a Standard Bearer at the same time. In addition, each unit can only upgrade models to a single Champion, a single Musician, and a single Standard Bearer.

Note that upgrading the unit with a Champion/Musician/Standard Bearer does not grant you extra models for the unit as you upgrade models that are already part of the unit.

Some Command Group models have additional options for upgrades, for instance the Standard Bearer in the example above can purchase a Banner Enchantment. These options are listed indented underneath the corresponding Command Group model. In order to have access to such an additional upgrade, you must first upgrade a model to the corresponding Command Group model, and only then you can buy the upgrade for that model.

11 – Unrestricted options

Many units have options to upgrade their models with weapons, armour, certain Model Rules, etc. In some cases, the Point Cost per unit is indicated, regardless of the number of models, while in others, like in the example above, the unit entry gives the Point Cost per model.

Note that if you choose to buy such an upgrade, you must always upgrade all models of the unit accordingly.

12 – Restricted options

Certain options may come with restrictions. These may for instance be associated with an altered maximum number of models per unit (in the example above 25 instead of 50), or with a restriction regarding the number of units with the upgrade an army may contain (up to 2 units in the example above). Another possible restriction is an upper limit on the total number of models with a given upgrade per army. In this case, the sum of all models of all units with that upgrade in the army may not exceed that upper limit.

Other options cannot be combined with one another. These are listed indented underneath "One choice only" in the unit entry. In the example above, the models in the unit may be upgraded either with Shields or with Paired Weapons, they may however not gain Shields and Paired Weapons.

In case there are several groups of these "One choice only" upgrades for a unit, the unit may be given up to one choice of each group.

13 – Model Rules

In case a unit profile contains any unit-specific Model Rules, these rules will be explained in this part of the unit entry.

8.D.b Complex Unit Entries

In addition to the elements detailed above, certain units may have additional distinctive features that will be explained based on the Character unit entry in figure 15.

Wicked Witch
140 pts

(a) single model   (b) 0–3 Units/Army

Height **Standard**
Type **Infantry**
Base **20×20 mm**

Global	Adv	Mar	Dis		Model Rules
	5"	10"	8		**Hydrophobe**, Wizard Apprentice

Defensive	HP	Def	Res	Arm
	3	4	3	0

Offensive	Att	Off	Str	AP	Agi
	1	4	3	0	5

— Magic Options — pts –

Wizard Adept   75
Wizard Master   225

(c) Cosmology   Druidism   Witchcraft

— Options — pts –

(d) Special Items   up to 100
   If Wizard Master   up to 200
   Red Rubber Boots   5

— Mount Options — pts –

(e) Witches' Broom   30
   Winged Monkey Chariot   200

— Model Rules —

Hydrophobe: Universal Rule.
   If the model touches a Water Terrain Feature, it is immediately removed as a casualty.

(f) — Optional Model Rules —

Red Rubber Boots: Universal Rule.
   The model loses the Hydrophobe Model Rule and gains Strider (Water Terrain).

Figure 15: Character unit entry.

a) Certain units, like Characters, consist only of a single model. These units are labelled as "single model" units. They follow the same rules as units consisting of multiple models, but there may be certain differences, like Characters being able to join other units.

b) Just like regular units, Characters may have a unit cap. This cap applies to all Characters of this type, regardless of their upgrades, equipment, and mounts. In this example, this means that you can only have up to 3 Wicked Witches in your army, e.g. one of them on foot and two on Witches' Brooms.

c) Models that can cast spells are referred to as Wizards. Wizards come in 3 different types: Wizard Apprentice, Adept, and Master. The Model Rules tell you which Wizard type the model has by default (in this example, the Wicked Witch is a Wizard Apprentice), while the Magic Options show you which types the model can be upgraded to. In case you upgrade your Wizard, the upgrade replaces the default Wizard type. In addition, you will also find in this section the Paths that the Wizard has to choose a single one from. The Wizard will select its spells from this chosen Path (see "Spell Selection", page 36).

d) Certain models, like most Characters, have access to Weapon Enchantments, Armour Enchantments, Artefacts, etc. These upgrades are referred to as Special Items (see "Special Items", page 116 and The 9th Age: Fantasy Battles – Arcane Compendium). If a model can buy Special Items, you will find this information in the unit entry's options, together with the maximum amount of points a model can spend on them.

e) Characters are usually on foot by default. Most of them can however be given a mount. The Mount Options will tell you which mounts are available for a Character and how many points you have to pay for them. Note that a Character may always only take a single mount.

f) As explained above, unit entries will contain unit-specific Model Rules. In addition, you will sometimes also find Optional Model Rules. In order to gain these Model Rules, you must buy the corresponding upgrade for the model.

8.D.c Unit Entries with Multipart Models

The examples above show entries of units with models consisting of a single model part, but there are also many Multipart Models in the game (see "Multipart Models", page 7). The unit entry of a Character Mount, the Winged Monkey Chariot from the example in figure 16, will be used to explain the particularities of this type of unit entry.

							Height **Large**
Winged Monkey Chariot					(a)		Type **Construct**
					0–1 Mounts/Army		Base **50×100 mm**

Global		Adv	Mar	Dis			Model Rules
	Ground	**2"**	**2"**	C	(b)		Fly (9", 9"), Light Troops, Swiftstride
	Fly	**9"**	**9"**				

Defensive	HP	Def	Res	Arm		
	4	**C**	**4**	**C+1**		Hard Target (1)

Offensive	Att	Off	Str	AP	Agi	
Crew (2)	**1**	**4**	**3**	**0**	**5**	Light Lance
Winged Monkey (2)	**2**	**4**	**4**	**1**	**4**	Harnessed, Hatred
Chassis			**5**	**2**		Impact Hits (D6), Inanimate

(c is marked to the left of the Offensive profile rows)

Figure 16: Unit entry of a Multipart Model.

a) Like for any other unit entry, there may be restrictions on the number of Character Mounts that can be part of an army. In the example above, the army may only contain up to a single Character, regardless of the type, on a Winged Monkey Chariot. This restriction only applies to Character mounts, so if an Army Book contains the Character mount additionally as a unit in another Army Category, you are allowed to take this unit in addition to the Character mount in your army.

b) In case of a Multipart Model Character, many of a model's Characteristic values will be determined by the mount's Characteristics, unless they are marked with "C" or "C+X" in the mount's profile (see "Special Cases of Characteristic Values", page 15), which refers to the value in the Character's profile. In this example, the mount does not have a proper Discipline Value, but the Multipart Model uses the Character's Discipline, which is 8.

c) Models consisting of a single model part have one Global, Defensive, and Offensive Profile each. Multipart Models also have one Global and Defensive Profile each, which apply to the entire Multipart Model. However, they do have a separate Offensive Profile for each identical model part. The mount above has 5 model parts: 2 Crew members and 2 Winged Monkey's (as indicated by the "2" in brackets) and a Chassis, which all have their own Offensive Profile.

8.E   Hidden and Open Lists

Rules are written and balanced based on the principle of openness, and we encourage players to share their full Army Lists with their opponents at the start of the game. This Army List should include all units, unit options, Special Items, special abilities, Point Costs, and so on. The only things that are not open to your opponent are things that are explicitly stated as hidden or secret.

8.E.a   Optional Rules for Hidden Lists

Some players may prefer to use so-called hidden lists, and for those players we have included the hidden list rules. Please note that the game is not balanced with these rules in mind. In this format, most of your Army List will be open, meaning that your opponent should know what your army consists of before the game starts. However, some parts of your army are secret or "hidden". Both players should provide their opponent with the open part of their army before the game begins, referred to as a mundane Army List.

The following elements are included in the hidden part of your army:

- Special Items that are picked from the List of Common Special Items given in The 9th Age: Fantasy Battles – Arcane Compendium

- Special Items that are specific to Army Books, as well as any option that follows the rules for Special Items such as Daemonic Items and Dwarven Runic Items

Anything not on this list belongs to the mundane Army List.

If an army has two or more units or models that are identical regarding their open part but have hidden differences, the player must be able to tell the units apart in the hidden list. For example if a player fields two units identical in every way except that one has an enchanted banner and the other doesn't, the Army List may specify that the unit with the enchanted banner has a red banner while the unit with a blue banner possesses no such Special Item.

8.E.a.1   Revealing Special Items

Special Items (or similar) must be revealed the first time they are used. A Special Item is considered as being used when it affects or could affect the game in any way. For example:

- It affects a dice roll (even if the actual result of the dice has no effect).

- It alters an attack (such as an enchanted weapon, or any Special Item with a rule that affects an attack).

- It alters a saving roll (reveal the Special Item before making the saving roll). Note that a Special Item that affects the saving roll the same way as the non-Enchanted counterpart would does not need to be revealed.

A Special Item that increases movement only counts as being used if the unit moves farther than it could without it or when Charging (declare that you have the Special Item before rolling the Charge Range but after Charge Reactions are resolved).

When revealing Dwarven Runic Items, only reveal the Rune that is being used, not the entire combined item.

9   Pre-Game Sequence

When setting up a game of The 9th Age: Fantasy Battles, players need to go through the following steps, referred to as the Pre-Game Sequence:

1	Decide on the size of the game
2	Share your Army List with your opponent
3	Build the Battlefield
4	Determine the Deployment Type
5	Determine the Secondary Objective
6	Determine the Deployment Zones
7	Select Spells
8	Declare Special Deployment
9	Deployment Phase

9.A   Size of the Game

In The 9th Age: Fantasy Battles, two armies opposing each other on the Battlefield must have roughly the same Point Cost. This is to ensure that the battle will be decided through clever strategies and tactics rather than unfair differences in army size.

The first step to setting up a game is to agree on the Army Points (see "Army Points", page 22), which will determine the size of the game. The size of the game is typically between 1500 and 3000 points for small engagements, between 3000 and 8000 points for serious battles, and beyond 8000 points for mighty clashes between epic armies. For an optimal gaming experience, we recommend playing at 4500 points.

9.B   Sharing Army Lists

After deciding on the size of the game, the next step is for both players to swap Army Lists and share all relevant information about the upcoming game.

Alternatively, players may agree to keep certain aspects about their armies secret, which they will progressively reveal during the course of the game. For more information please see "Optional Rules for Hidden Lists", page 31.

9.C Building the Battlefield

The 9th Age: Fantasy Battles is intended to be played on a board that is 72″ wide and 48″ deep. For smaller battles involving Warbands, we recommend playing on a board that is 36″ wide and 48″ deep (half the standard board), while for bigger games involving Grand Armies we recommend that the players increase the size of the board as they see fit in order to accommodate the larger armies.

While some battles may take place on a completely open board, a Battlefield typically has Terrain Features placed upon it (see "Terrain", page 89). These pieces of Terrain could represent exactly what they are, but they could also be representations of far greater things for the purpose of the game. So a copse of trees could represent a forest, a stream could actually be a wide river, a single house could denote a hamlet, and a tower could represent a keep. The players can freely agree on the size, type, and number of Terrain Features to be placed, as well as their positions. If an agreement cannot be reached, the game provides the following default rules for setting up a randomly generated Battlefield.

1	Divide the board into 24×24″ sections (18×24″ if the board is 36×48″).
2	Place the following Terrain Features in the centre of three different randomly selected sections: • One Impassable Terrain • One Hill • One Forest
3	Move each Terrain Feature 2D6″ in a random direction.
4	Add 2D3 additional Terrain Features in the centre of different randomly selected sections (1D3 if the board is 36×48″, 3D3 or more for boards larger than 72×48″). Roll 2D6 and consult the table below to determine the type of each additional Terrain Feature.
5	Move each additional Terrain Feature 2D6″ in a random direction.

2–4	5	6	7	8	9–10	11–12
Hill	Water Terrain	Field	Forest	Ruins	Impassable Terrain	Wall

- Terrain Features cannot be moved to be closer than 6″ from each other. You may move them as little as possible from their rolled position in order to meet this criterion. If it is not possible to place the Terrain Feature more than 6″ away from any other Terrain then discard the problematic piece.

- Recommended Terrain Feature sizes are between 6×8″ and 6×10″, except for Walls, which are 1×8″, and Impassable Terrain, which is between 6×6″ and 6×8″.

9.D Deployment Types

If no outside source tells you what Deployment Type to use (e.g. tournament organiser, campaign rules, etc.), players may agree on a Deployment Type. Otherwise randomise by rolling a D6 and consulting the list below.

Certain Deployment Types refer to the Centre Line. This is the line drawn through the centre of the board and parallel to the long Board Edges, dividing the board into halves.

1: Frontline Clash

Deployment Zones are areas more than 12″ away from the Centre Line.

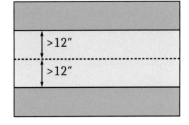

2: Dawn Assault

The player choosing the Deployment Zone also chooses a short Board Edge and the other player gets the opposite short Board Edge. Deployment Zones are areas more than 12″ away from the Centre Line and more than 1/4 of the board's length from the opponent's short Board Edge (18″ on a 72″ board). When declaring Special Deployment, players may choose to keep up to two of their units as reinforcement. These units follow the rules for Ambushing units, except that they must be placed touching the owner's short Board Edge when they arrive.

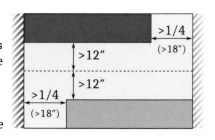

3: Counterthrust

Deployment Zones are areas more than 8″ away from the Centre Line. Units must be deployed more than 20″ away from enemy units. During their first 3 deployment turns, each player must deploy a single unit, and cannot deploy any Characters.
Units using Special Deployment, such as Scout, ignore these restrictions and follow their Special Deployment rules.

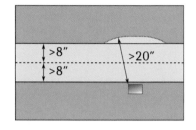

4: Encircle

The player choosing the Deployment Zone decides if they want to be the attacker or the defender. The attacker must deploy more than 9″ from the Centre Line if entirely within a quarter of the board's length from either short Board Edge (18″ on a 72″ board), and more than 15″ from the Centre Line elsewhere. The defender does the opposite: more than 15″ away from the Centre Line if within a quarter of the board's length from the short Board Edge, and more than 9″ away from the Centre Line elsewhere.

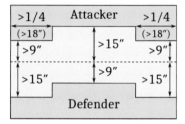

5: Refused Flank

The board is divided into halves by a diagonal line across the board. Whoever gets to choose the Deployment Zone decides which diagonal to use. Deployment Zones are areas more than 9″ away from this line.

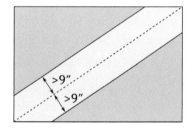

6: Marching Columns

Deployment Zones are areas more than 12″ away from the Centre Line.
Each player must choose a short Board Edge when deploying their first unit. Each unit this player deploys afterwards must be deployed with its Centre farther away from the chosen short Board Edge than the Centre of the last unit this player deployed (measure from the closest point on the short Board Edge). Characters, War Machines, War Platforms, and Scouting units ignore these rules.
During their first 3 deployment turns, each player must deploy a single unit, and cannot deploy any Characters, War Machines, or War Platforms.
Instead of deploying a unit, a player may choose to make all their undeployed units Delayed that are not using Special Deployment. Delayed units follow the rules for Ambushing units with the following exceptions:

- In each Player Turn, after rolling for all Ambushing units, the Reactive Player chooses the order in which all Delayed units that passed the 3+ roll enter the Battlefield.
- In the chosen order, each unit must be placed one after the other with the centre of its rear rank as close as possible to the centre of the long Board Edge in their owner's Deployment Zone, before any non-Delayed Ambushers are placed on the Battlefield.
- After all arriving units have been placed, they can be moved as described in the rules for Ambush (see page 93).

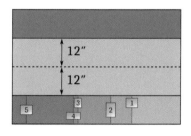

9.E   Secondary Objectives

Once the Deployment Type is established, determine the Secondary Objective. If no outside source tells you which one to use (e.g. tournament organiser, campaign rule, etc.), players may agree on a Secondary Objective. Otherwise, randomise by rolling a D6 and consulting the list below. See "Victory Conditions", page 85 for more details on how capturing an objective affects who is the winner.

1: Hold the Ground

Secure and hold the centre of Battlefield.
Mark the centre of the board.

At the end of each Game Turn after the first, the player with the most Scoring Units within 6" of the centre of the board gains a counter. At the end of the game, the player with the most such counters wins this Secondary Objective.

2: Breakthrough

Invade the enemy territory.
The player with the most Scoring Units inside their opponent's Deployment Zone at the end of the game, up to a maximum of 3, wins this Secondary Objective.

3: Spoils of War

Gather precious loot.
Place 3 markers along the line dividing the board into halves (the dashed line in the figures describing Deployment Types). One marker is placed with its centre on a point on this line that is as close as possible to the centre of the board while still being more than 1" away from Impassable Terrain. The other two markers are placed with their centres on points on this line that are on either side of the central marker, as close to the centre of the board as possible but at least a third of the length of the long Board Edge (24" on a standard board) away from it, and more than 1" away from Impassable Terrain.

At the start of each of your Player Turns, each of your Scoring units that is not carrying a marker may pick up a single marker whose centre they are in contact with. Remove the marker from the Battlefield: the unit is now carrying the marker. Units carrying a marker with less than 3 Full Ranks cannot perform March Moves. If a unit carrying a marker is destroyed or loses Scoring, the opponent must immediately place the marker carried by this unit with its centre on a point within 3" of it. Ignore Post-Combat Reform for this purpose. This point cannot be within 1" of Impassable Terrain, but it can be inside a unit.

At the end of the game, the player with the most units carrying markers wins this Secondary Objective.

4: King of the Hill

Desecrate your opponent's holy ground while protecting yours.
After Spell Selection (at the end of step 7 of the Pre-Game Sequence), both players choose a Terrain Feature that isn't Impassable Terrain and that is not fully inside their Deployment Zone, starting with the player that chose their Deployment Zone (note that both players may choose the same Terrain Feature).

A player captures their opponent's chosen Terrain Feature if any of the player's Scoring Units are inside that Terrain Feature at the end of the game. If a player captures their opponent's chosen Terrain Feature while not allowing their own to be captured, they win this Secondary Objective.

5: Capture the Flags

Valuable targets must be annihilated.
After Spell Selection (at the end of step 7 of the Pre-Game Sequence), mark all Scoring Units on both players' Army Lists. If either player has less than 3 marked units, their opponent must mark enough units from this player's Army List so that there are exactly 3 marked units in the army, starting with the player that chose their Deployment Zone.

The player that has the lowest number of their marked units removed as casualties at the end of the game wins this Secondary Objective.

6: Secure Target

Critical resources must not fall into enemy hands.
Directly after determining Deployment Zones, both players place one marker on the Battlefield, starting with the player that chose their Deployment Zone. Each player must place the marker with its centre on a point that is more than 12″ away from their Deployment Zone and a third of the long Board Edge length (24″ on a standard board) from the point marked by the other marker.

At the end of the game, the player controlling the most markers wins this Secondary Objective. A marker is controlled by the player with the most Scoring Units within 6″ of the centre of the marker. If a unit is within 6″ of the centres of both markers, it only counts as within 6″ of the centre of the marker which is closest to its Centre (randomise if both markers' centres are equally close).

9.F   Deployment Zones

After the Secondary Objective is determined, both players roll a D6. The player that rolls higher chooses their Deployment Zone and follows the Deployment Type specific instructions if applicable. In case of a tie, roll again.

9.G   Spell Selection

Starting with the player that chose their Deployment Zone, each player must now select spells for their Wizards, one at a time. All Magic Paths can be found in The 9th Age: Fantasy Battles – Arcane Compendium. Hereditary Spells can be found in the corresponding Army Books.

9.G.a   Wizard Apprentice

- Knows **1 spell**
- Can select between the Learned Spell **1** of its chosen Path and the **Hereditary** Spell of its army

9.G.b   Wizard Adept

- Knows **2** different **spells**
- Can select from the Learned Spells **1, 2, 3, and 4** of its chosen Path and the **Hereditary** Spell of its army

9.G.c   Wizard Master

- Knows **4** different **spells**
- Can select from the Learned Spells **1, 2, 3, 4, 5, and 6** of its chosen Path and the **Hereditary** Spell of its army

9.H   Declaring Special Deployment

Starting with the player that chose their Deployment Zone, each player must nominate which units with Special Deployment options (such as Scout or Ambush) will use their Special Deployment, or if they will deploy using the normal rules.

10 Deployment Phase

10.A Deployment Phase Sequence

1	Determine who deploys first
2	Take turns deploying units
3	Declare intent to go first or second
4	Deploy remaining units
5	Deploy Scouting units (starting with the player who finished deploying first)
6	Move Vanguarding units (starting with the player who finished deploying last)
7	Other rules and abilities
8	Roll for first turn

10.B Determine Who Deploys First

The player who did not choose the Deployment Zone decides which player deploys first.

10.C Deploy Units

The players then take turns deploying their units fully inside their own Deployment Zone. On each of their deployment turns, a player can deploy any number of units, but must deploy at least one unit. All Characters count as a single unit during the Deployment Phase and must all be deployed during the same deployment turn.

10.D Declare Intent to Go First or Second

Once a player has deployed all of their units (excluding units that are deployed with alternative rules, such as Ambushing or Scouting units), that player must announce whether they will play first or second should they win the Roll for First Turn.

10.E Deploy Remaining Units

The other player must now deploy the rest of their units. The number of units deployed in this step is called the Undeployed Units Number and will be used in the Roll for First Turn. As before, all remaining Characters count as one unit when deployed.

10.E.a Undeployable Units

In the unlikely event that a unit cannot be deployed during the Deployment Phase for whatever reason (e.g. if there is not enough space in the player's Deployment Zone), the unit counts as destroyed, unless specifically stated otherwise.

10.F Deploy Scouting Units

Both players deploy their units that have been nominated to use their Scout rules during "Declaring Special Deployment", page 36, starting with the player who first completed their normal deployment (see "Scout", page 98).

10.G   Move Vanguarding Units

Both players move their units with Vanguard (see "Vanguard (X)", page 100), starting with the player who finished deploying last.

10.H   Other Rules And Abilities

Put into effect all rules and abilities described as taking place right before the battle.

10.I   Roll For First Turn

Both players must now roll a D6. The player that finished deploying first adds the Undeployed Units Number to their dice roll.

- If the player who finished deploying first scores a higher result, they play first or second, whichever they previously declared.
- If the score is a tie or the player who finished deploying second scores a higher result, that player can now choose which player has the first turn.

11   Charge Phase

The Charge Phase is when the Active Player has the chance to move their units into combat with enemy units. Declaring a Charge and then performing a successful Charge Move is usually the only way to engage an enemy unit in combat.

11.A   Charge Phase Sequence

The Charge Phase is divided into the following steps:

1	Start of the Charge Phase (and start of the Player Turn)
2	The Active Player chooses a unit and declares a Charge
3	The Reactive Player declares and resolves their Charge Reaction
4	Repeat steps 2–3 of this sequence until all units that wish to declare a Charge have done so
5	The Active Player chooses a unit that declared a Charge, then rolls for Charge Range, and moves the unit
6	Repeat step 5 of this sequence until all units that declared a Charge have moved
7	End of the Charge Phase

See figures 22 and 23, page 48 and 49, for the illustration of a Charge Phase with several units Charging enemy units and those enemy units declaring and performing their Charge Reactions.

11.B   Declaring Charges

Select one of your units that is not already Charging, Engaged in Combat, Fleeing, or contains any Shaken models and declare which enemy unit it will Charge. Each time the Active Player declares a Charge, the Reactive Player must declare the Charged unit's Charge Reaction. In order to be able to declare a Charge:

- At least one model in the Charging unit's first rank must be able to draw Line of Sight to the Charged unit's Unit Boundary.

- The Charged unit must be within the Charging unit's maximum potential Charge Range (which usually is the Charging unit's Advance Rate + 12″).

- There must be enough room to move the Charging unit into base contact with the Charged unit.

When determining if there is enough room for the Charging unit:

- Take into account already declared Charges (including align moves of Charging and Charged units)

- Do not take into account any potential Flee Charge Reactions (including mandatory ones)

- Do not take into account any potential casualties inflicted to the Charging unit (e.g. by Stand and Shoot Charge Reactions or failed Dangerous Terrain Tests)

- Do not take into account any potential Combat Reforms due to Blocked Path

The unit declaring a Charge is now considered Charging until it has:

- Finished its First Round of Combat after making a Charge Move

- Successfully Charged a Fleeing unit

- Performed a Failed Charge Move

- Failed a Panic Test before completing the Charge Move

- Been subject to the rules for No Longer Engaged

11.C Charge Reactions

Before declaring a Charge Reaction, determine in which Facing the unit will be Charged. This is determined by the unit's Arc which the Charging unit is Located in (see figure 17).

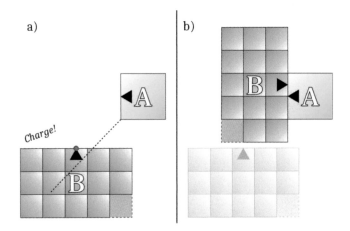

Figure 17: Front or Flank?

a) The Charging unit is Located in the enemy's Front Arc (since this is where the centre of its Front Facing is).

b) The Charging unit must contact the Charged unit's Front Facing.

A unit must declare and then resolve its Charge Reaction immediately after a Charge is declared against it and the Facing in which it will be Charged is determined, before any further Charges are declared. There are three different Charge Reactions: "Hold", "Stand and Shoot", and "Flee".

11.C.a Hold

A Hold Charge Reaction means that the unit does nothing.

Units Engaged in Combat can only choose to declare the Hold Charge Reaction.

11.C.b Stand and Shoot

A Stand and Shoot Charge Reaction means that the Charged unit immediately performs a Shooting Attack as if in the Shooting Phase, even if the enemy is beyond the attack's maximum range. In this case, the Charging unit is considered to be at Long Range for the Shooting Attack. Remember to apply any modifiers like Long Range and Stand and Shoot. After this, follow the rules for Hold Charge Reactions.

A Stand and Shoot Charge Reaction can only be taken if all of the following conditions are met:

- The Charged unit can perform Shooting Attacks.
- The Charging unit is Located in the Charged unit's Front Arc.
- The Charging unit is farther away than its Advance Rate; use the lowest value among the Charging models if it has more than one.

Units can only choose to declare a Stand and Shoot Charge Reaction once per Player Turn (even if they are Charged more than once).

11.C.c Flee

A Flee Charge Reaction means that the Charged unit starts Fleeing. It is immediately Pivoted to face directly away from the Charging enemy (along a line drawn from the Centre of the Charging unit through the Centre of the Charged unit) and performs a Flee Move (see "Flee Moves", page 50). After a unit completes this Flee Move, any unit that declared a Charge against this unit may immediately attempt to Redirect the Charge.

If the Fleeing unit's Front Facing comes into contact with any unit that declared a Charge against it in this phase (regardless whether the enemy unit Redirected its Charge), the Fleeing unit is removed as a casualty.

Units already Fleeing when Charged can only choose to declare a Flee Charge Reaction.

11.D Redirecting a Charge

After a unit declares a Flee Charge Reaction, the Charging unit may attempt to Redirect the Charge by rolling a Discipline Test. If failed, the unit will try to complete the Charge against the unit that Fled. If passed, the unit may immediately declare a new Charge against another viable target unit, which may choose their Charge Reaction as normal. If more than one unit declared a Charge against the Fleeing unit, each may attempt to Redirect the Charge in any order chosen by the Active Player. If a unit Redirects a Charge and the second target also Flees, the Charging unit may opt to Charge either target, but must declare which before rolling the Charge Range.

Units can only attempt to Redirect a Charge once per Player Turn.

11.E Move Chargers

After all Charges have been declared and all Charge Reactions have been declared and completed, Chargers will attempt to move into combat. Choose a unit that has declared a Charge in this phase, roll its Charge Range, and then perform the Charge Move. Repeat these steps with all units that have declared a Charge in this phase.

11.E.a Charge Range

A unit's Charge Range is normally 2D6″ plus the unit's Advance Rate, using the lowest Advance Rate among the unit's models.

- If the Charge Range is **equal to or higher** than the distance between the Charger and the Charged unit, and if there is enough space to complete the Charge, the Charge is successful and the Charger performs a Charge Move.

- If the Charge Range is less than the distance between the Charger and the Charged unit, or if there is not enough space to complete the Charge (see "Impossible Charge", page 46), the Charge has failed and the Charger performs a Failed Charge Move.

11.E.b Charge Move

A Charge Move is resolved as follows:

- The unit can move forwards an unlimited distance.
- A single Wheel can be performed during the move (remember a Wheel may not exceed 90°).
- The Front Facing of the Charging unit must contact the Charged unit in the Arc determined when declaring the Charge Reaction.
- The Charging unit is allowed to come within 0.5″ of other units and Impassable Terrain as per the Unit Spacing rule. It can only move into base contact with an enemy unit that it declared a Charge against (remember that it is allowed to come into base contact with friendly units and Impassable Terrain).

11.E.c Aligning Units

After the Charger manages to move into base contact with the Charged unit, the units must now be aligned towards each other. An align move is performed as follows:

1	The Active Player rotates the Charging unit around the point where it contacted the enemy (see figure 17), so that the Charging unit's Front Facing and the Charged unit's Facing in which it was contacted are parallel.
2	If this will not align the two units properly, for example due to interfering Terrain or other units, players may rotate the Charged unit instead if this will achieve proper contact between them, or do a combination of the two, rotating the enemy unit as little as possible.

The Charged unit must only be moved if it is the only way to align the units. Units can never be moved if they are already Engaged in Combat. These moves are considered part of the Charge Move, so they may bring the units within 0.5″ of other units and Impassable Terrain as per the Unit Spacing rule. A unit that is forced to make an align move when it is Charged never has to take Dangerous Terrain Tests due to this move.

11.E.d Maximising Contact

Charge Moves must be made so the following conditions are satisfied as best as possible, in decreasing priority order.

- 1st priority: Make contact with no enemy units other than the one that was Charged. If it will be unavoidable to make contact with more than one enemy unit, make contact with as few enemy units as possible. Follow the rules for Multiple Charges.

- 2nd priority: Maximise the total number of Charging units that make contact (note that this is only applicable when multiple units Charge the same unit).

- 3rd priority: Avoid rotating the Charged unit (see "Aligning Units", page 41). If it is unavoidable, rotate the unit as little as possible. Remember that units Engaged in Combat cannot be rotated.

- 4th priority: Maximise the number of models (on both sides) in base contact with at least one enemy model (including models fighting across gaps).

See figure 18 for an example.

If it is unavoidable to break one or more of the above conditions, you must avoid breaking the higher priority order conditions, even if this means the total number of conditions you break is higher. As long as all above conditions are satisfied as best is possible, Charging units are free to move as they please (following the rules for Moving Chargers).

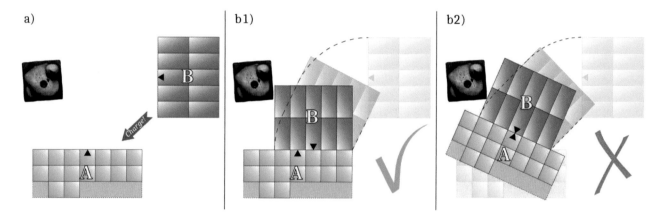

Figure 18: Maximising contact.

a) Unit B Charges an enemy unit. Follow the priority order given by Maximising Contact when moving the Charger.
1. Not Charging multiple enemy units
2. Maximising the number of units Engaged in Combat
3. Not rotating the enemy unit
4. Maximising the number of models in contact with one or more enemy models

b1) OK.
1. Not applicable
2. Not applicable
3. The Charged unit is not rotated
4. The number of models is maximised without breaking priority 3. A total of 11 (5 vs 6) models is in base contact with one or more enemy models

b2) Not OK.
1. Not applicable
2. Not applicable
3. The Charged unit is rotated. The Charge is illegal
4. The number of models is maximised. A total of 12 (5 vs 7) models is in base contact with one or more enemy models, which is more than b1). This is irrelevant though since the Charge is illegal due to the Charged unit being rotated

11.E.e Multiple Charges

If it will be unavoidable for a Charging unit to contact more than one enemy unit during the Charge Move, the rules for Multiple Charges are applied when declaring Charges:

- First declare a Charge against a single initial target as normal.

- If the initial target of the Charge declares a Charge Reaction other than Flee, the Charging unit must, after the initial target has declared and resolved its Charge Reaction, successively declare secondary Charges against all enemy units it cannot avoid contacting, in an order chosen by the Active Player.

- The targets of secondary Charges declare and perform Charge Reactions as normal.

- If the initial target of the Charge Flees or is destroyed before the Charging unit is moved, ignore all secondary Charges and treat the Charge as a normal Charge against the initial target only.

- If a target of a secondary Charge Flees, the Charging unit is not allowed to redirect the Charge, unless the initial target also Flees.

- If a Multiple Charge no longer is unavoidable after all Charges have been declared and after all Charge Reactions have been performed, ignore all secondary Charges and treat the Charge as a normal Charge against the initial target only.

Note that if contacting more than one enemy unit becomes unavoidable only after all Charges have been declared and all Charge Reactions have been performed, the rules for Multiple Charges do not apply and the Charging unit performs a Failed Charge Move.

See figure 19 for examples in which the rules for Multiple Charges apply.

11.E.f Combined Charges

When more than one unit has declared a Charge against the same enemy unit, Chargers are moved in a slightly different order:

1	Roll Charge Range for each unit Charging that same unit before moving any of them.
2	Check which units would be able to reach their target (sufficiently high Charge Range rolls, no other units blocking the Charge Move, etc.).
3	Perform the Charge Moves of all Charging units (including those failing their Charge) in the order that best satisfies the priority order of the Maximising Contact rule.

See figure 20 for an example.

11.E.g Engaged in Combat

As soon as a unit completes a Charge, it is Engaged in Combat: units are considered Engaged in Combat (or short Engaged) as long as one or more models in the unit are in base contact and aligned with an enemy unit. In addition, if a unit is Engaged at the start of a Round of Combat, it counts as Engaged until the start of step 7 of the Round of Combat Sequence (before calculating Combat Score and taking Break Tests, even if it loses base contact with all enemy units before then).

If a unit is Engaged in Combat, all models in the unit are also considered to be Engaged in Combat. Units that are Engaged in Combat cannot move unless specifically stated otherwise (such as during Combat Reforms or when Breaking from Combat).

11.E.h Charging a Fleeing Unit

When Charging a Fleeing unit, follow the rules for Charge Moves, except that the Charging unit can move into contact with any Facing of the Charged unit. Do not align or maximise base contact. Once the Charger makes contact with the Fleeing unit, the Fleeing unit is removed as a casualty. Once the Fleeing unit has been removed, the Charging unit can take a Discipline Test. If the test it passed, the unit may perform a Post-Combat Pivot manoeuvre.

A unit that has Charged a Fleeing unit is Shaken until the end of the Player Turn.

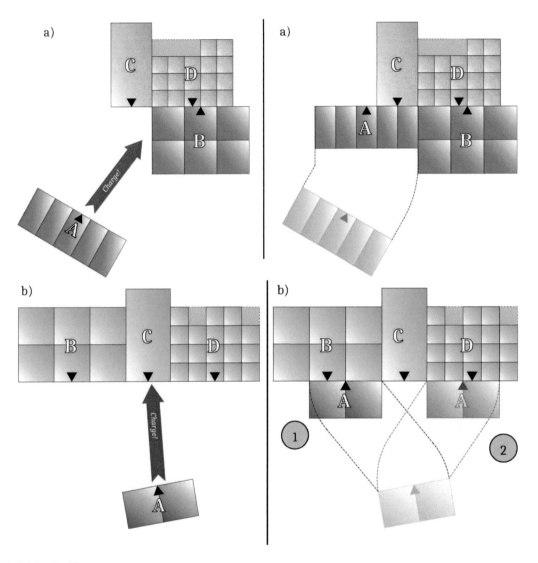

Figure 19: Multiple Charges.

a) When Charging unit D in the Front Facing, unit A cannot avoid contacting unit C, so the rules for Multiple Charges apply. Unit A declares a Charge against D as its initial target and a secondary Charge against C. Both Charged units have to Hold as they are already Engaged in Combat.

b) Units B, C, and D are aligned and in base contact with one another (this situation may arise if all 3 units had previously Charged and destroyed an enemy unit). Unit A cannot avoid contacting more than one enemy unit when charging unit C, so the rules for Multiple Charges apply. As per the rules for Maximising Contact as few enemy units as possible must be contacted (1st priority), so A must declare a secondary Charge against either unit B or unit D. In case neither unit C nor the target of the secondary Charge Flee as a Charge Reaction, A moves into contact with both units, maximising the number of models in base contact according to the 4th priority (position 1 in case unit B was Charged, position 2 in case unit D was Charged).

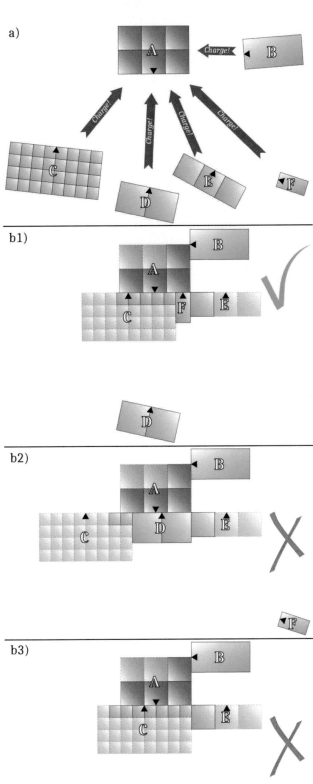

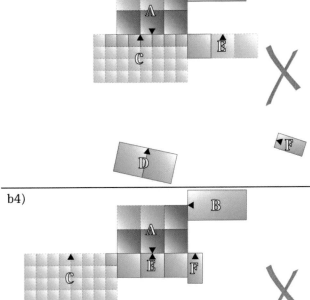

Figure 20: Combined Charges.

a) Multiple units declaring a Charge against a single unit. Follow the priority order given by Maximising Contact.

    1. Not Charging multiple enemy units

    2. Maximising the number of Charging units in the combat

    3. Not rotating the Charged unit

    4. Maximising the number of models in contact with one or more enemy models

b1) OK

    1. Not applicable

    2. Maximised. 4 Charging units are Engaged (unit A's Front Facing is only wide enough for 3 of the 4 Charging units in the Front Arc)

    3. Not applicable

    4. Maximised without breaking priority 2. A total of 12 (4 vs 8) models is in contact with one or more enemy models. Notice that the flanking unit is only in contact with one enemy model. This is allowed because other models it could contact are already in contact with enemy models

b2) Not OK

    1. Not applicable

    2. Maximised. 4 Charging units are Engaged

    3. Not applicable

    4. Not maximised. A total of 10 (4 vs 6) models is in contact with one or more enemy models

b3) Not OK

    1. Not applicable

    2. Not maximised. Only 3 Charging units are Engaged. The Charge is illegal

    3. Not applicable

    4. Maximised. A total of 13 (4 vs 9) models is in contact with one or more enemy models, which is more than all the above. This is irrelevant though since the Charge is illegal due to the number of units not being maximised

b4) Not OK

    1. Not applicable

    2. Maximised. 4 Charging units are Engaged

    3. Not applicable

    4. Not maximised. A total of 10 (4 vs 6) models is in contact with one or more enemy models. The Charge is illegal

11.E.i Impossible Charge

Sometimes units block each other from reaching combat when moving the Chargers (or there is not enough space to fit all Chargers). When this happens, the units that can no longer make it into combat must make a Failed Charge Move.

11.E.j Failed Charge

When a unit does not roll a sufficient Charge Range, or is otherwise unable to complete the Charge, it performs a Failed Charge Move, comprising an initial Wheel and a subsequent straight forward move, as follows:

1	The move distance of a Failed Charge Move is equal to the highest D6 of the Charge Range roll.
2	Wheel the unit until it is facing directly towards the Centre of its intended target or if it was destroyed, towards the final position of the Centre of the unit, or until it cannot Wheel anymore due to obstructions (whichever comes first).
3	Move the unit straight forward the remaining move distance.

A Failed Charge Move may bring the unit within 0.5″ of other units and Impassable Terrain as per the Unit Spacing rule.

Models in a unit that performs a Failed Charge Move are Shaken until the end of the Player Turn. Units that have completed a Failed Charge Move are no longer considered Charging.

11.E.k Blocked Path

To prevent abusive situations where a unit cannot Charge an enemy unit well within Charge Range and Line of Sight due to a convoluted positioning of enemy units, potentially in conjunction with Impassable Terrain, the following rules are applied.

If, after declaring a Charge, a unit is unable to complete the Charge solely due to unengaged enemy units that it could not Charge (normally), or due to the combination of at least two unengaged enemy units and one or more Impassable Terrain Features, it can make a special Charge Move as described below.

Move the unit straight forward up to its Charge Range. If this brings the Charging unit into base contact with the enemy unit against which the Charge was declared, that unit is Charged. Instead of Aligning Units as normal, the enemy unit performs a Combat Reform to bring the units into alignment with each other (see "Combat Reforms", page 79). Combat Reform so that:

- The Charged Facing determined when declaring the Charge Reaction is aligned with the Charging unit.
- The Charging unit is Engaged in its Front Facing.
- The Charged unit does not change its number of ranks or files.
- The number of models (on both sides) in base contact with an enemy is maximised.

If it is not possible to align the units without changing the number of ranks or files, you may change the number of ranks and files and do not have to maximise models in base contact. If the enemy unit is unable to perform a Combat Reform to align the units, the Blocked Path Charge Move cannot be performed.

Figure 21 illustrates Blocked Path situations.

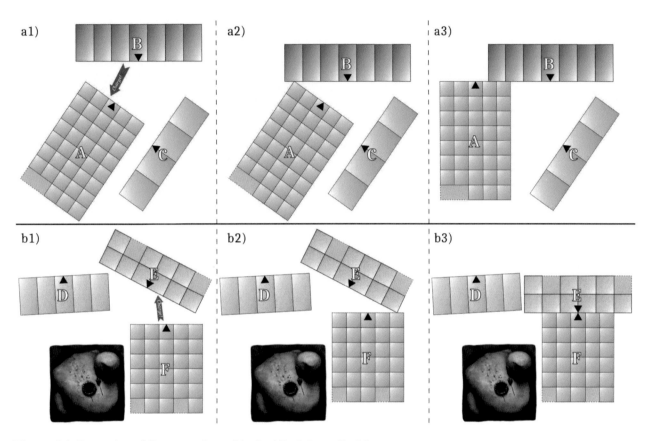

Figure 21: Examples of Charges where Blocked Path is applicable.

a1) Unit B Charges unit A, but the units cannot be aligned towards each other, solely due to the enemy unit C.
a2) Unit B performs a Blocked Path move: it moves forwards until it contacts unit A.
a3) Unit A then performs a Combat Reform to align the units.
b1) Unit F Charges unit E, but the units cannot be aligned towards each other due to the enemy unit D and the Impassable Terrain.
b2) Unit F performs a Blocked Path move: it moves forwards until it contacts unit E.
b3) Unit E then performs a Combat Reform to align the units.

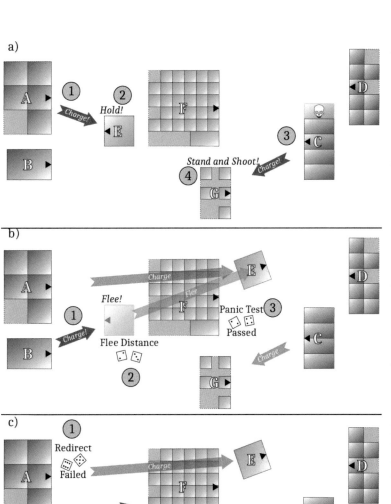

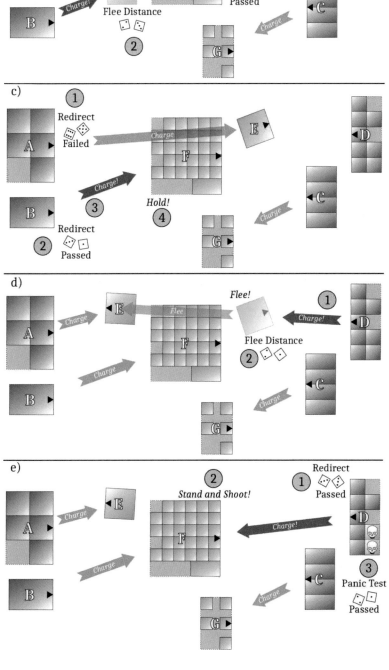

Figure 22: Example of a Charge Phase involving multiple units.

a) 1. Unit A declares a Charge against unit E.
2. Unit E declares and resolves a Hold Charge Reaction.
3. Unit C declares a Charge against unit G.
4. Unit G declares and resolves a Stand and Shoot Charge Reaction, inflicting 1 casualty against unit C.

b) 1. Unit B declares a Charge against unit E.
2. Unit E declares and resolves a Flee Charge Reaction, rolling 5″ for the Flee Distance. The Flee Move would make unit E end its move inside unit F's Unit Boundary, so the Flee Distance is extended for unit E to get clear of unit F.
3. Unit F takes a Panic Test for the friendly unit E Fleeing through its Unit Boundary and passes the test.

c) 1. Since unit E performed a Flee Charge Reaction, unit A may attempt to Redirect the Charge. The unit however fails the Discipline Test, so it must try to complete the Charge against unit E.
2. Unit B also attempts to Redirect the Charge and passes the Discipline Test. Unit B now declares a Charge against unit F.
3. Unit F declares and performs a Hold Charge Reaction.

d) 1. Unit D declares a Charge against the Fleeing unit E. Note that this Charge is legal although at this point unit D could not complete this Charge as unit C would block the Charge Move, because already declared Charges are taken into account when determining if there is enough room for a Charging unit to complete the Charge.
2. Since unit E is already Fleeing, it must declare and perform another Flee Charge Reaction, rolling 3″ for the Flee Distance. As before, the Flee Distance is extended until unit E gets clear of unit F. Unit F does not take a Panic Test for a friendly unit Fleeing through its Unit Boundary as it already passed a Panic Test during this phase.

e) 1. Unit D attempts to Redirect the Charge and passes the Discipline Test. Unit D declares a Charge against unit F.
2. Unit F declares and performs a Stand and Shoot Charge Reaction, inflicting 2 casualties against unit D.
3. Unit D takes and passes a Panic Test for losing 25% or more Health Points.

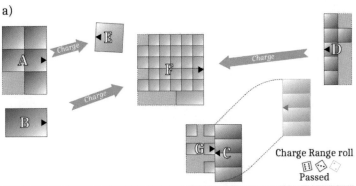

Figure 23: Example of a Charge Phase involving multiple units – part 2.

After all Charges have been declared and all Charge Reactions have been declared and performed, the Active Player moves all the units that declared Charges this turn, by rolling a unit's Charge Range and then moving the unit, in an order chosen by the Active Player.

a) Unit C rolls a sufficiently high Charge Range to reach unit G. Unit C performs a Charge Move against unit G.

b) Unit A rolls a sufficiently high Charge Range to reach the Fleeing unit E. Unit A performs a Charge Move against unit E. Since unit E was Fleeing, it is removed as a casualty as soon as the Charging unit moves into contact (without aligning or maximising base contact).

c) Unit A performs and passes a Discipline Test in order to perform a Post-Combat Pivot after successfully Charging a Fleeing unit.

d) Since units B and D both Charge the same enemy unit, both units roll their Charge Range before any of the units that are part of the Combined Charge is moved. Unit B rolls a sufficiently high Charge Range, while unit D fails the Charge Range roll.

e) Unit B performs a Charge Move against unit F, following the rules for "Maximising Contact", page 42. Unit D performs a Failed Charge Move towards unit F.

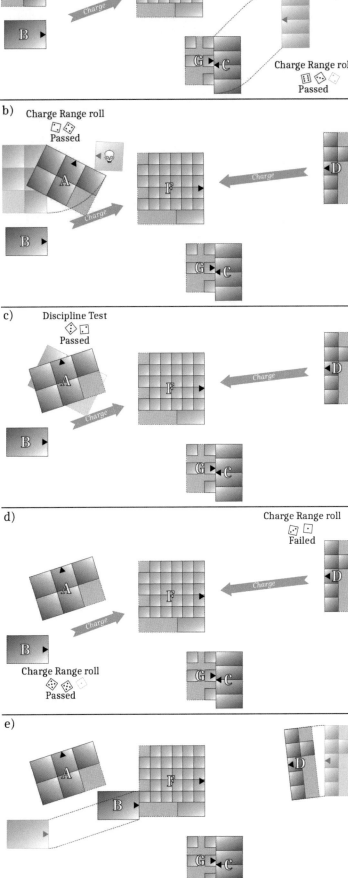

12 Movement Phase

In the Movement Phase you have the chance to move your units on the Battlefield.

12.A Movement Phase Sequence

The Movement Phase is divided into the following steps:

1	Start of the Movement Phase
2	Rally Fleeing units and perform any Flee Moves
3	Moving Units: Select one of your units, take a March Test if necessary, select a type of move (Advance, March, Reform), then move the unit
4	Repeat step 3, each time choosing a new unit that has not yet moved in the Movement Phase
5	End of the Movement Phase

12.B Rallying Fleeing Units

In an order chosen by the Active Player, each friendly unit that was Fleeing at the start of the Player Turn must take a Discipline Test, called a Rally Test:

- If the test is passed, the unit is no longer considered Fleeing and must immediately perform a Reform; models in the unit are Shaken until the end of the Player Turn.

- If the test is failed, the unit immediately performs a Flee Move (straight forward).

Note that if the unit is Decimated (see "Decimated", page 84), the Rally Test will be taken at half Discipline, rounding fractions up.

12.C Flee Moves

A Flee Move is performed as follows:

1	Roll the Flee Distance, which is normally 2D6″.
2	Move the Fleeing unit this distance straight forward.

- If the Flee Move takes the Fleeing unit into contact with the Board Edge, remove the unit as a casualty as soon as it touches the Board Edge (possibly causing Panic Tests to nearby units).

- If this move would make the Fleeing unit end its move within 1″ of another unit's Unit Boundary or Impassable Terrain, extend the Flee Distance by the minimum distance required for the unit to get clear of all such obstructions.

- If this move would make the Fleeing unit end its move inside another unit's Unit Boundary or inside Impassable Terrain, extend the Flee Distance by the minimum distance required for the unit to get clear of all such obstructions.

- If Fleeing models move through the Unit Boundary of an enemy unit or Impassable Terrain, they must take a Dangerous Terrain (3) Test (see "Dangerous Terrain (X)", page 89).

- If Fleeing models move through a friendly unit's Unit Boundary, that unit must take a Panic Test.

Note that Flee Moves are often preceded by a Pivot. This Pivot follows the same rules as the Flee Move.

12.D   Moving Units

Choose one of your units to move that is not Charging, Engaged in Combat, Fleeing, or contains any Shaken models.

Then perform a March Test if necessary and choose what type of move this unit will perform, and move the unit. The different types of move are Advance Move, March Move, and Reform. In order to affect a unit's movement, effects (like Universal Rules or movement modifiers) need to be present at the start of the unit's movement.

Repeat this process, each time choosing a new unit that has not yet moved in the Movement Phase. Once all units that can move (and want to) have done so, the Movement Phase ends.

12.D.a   March Test

Just before moving a unit, if it is within 8″ of any non-Fleeing enemy units, the unit must take a Discipline Test, called March Test:

- If the test is passed, the unit may proceed as normal.
- If the test is failed, the unit cannot perform a March Move during this Movement Phase (it can perform any other type of move as normal, or choose not to move at all).

12.D.b   Advance Move

When performing an Advance Move, a unit can move forwards, backwards, or sideways, but it cannot move in more than one of these directions during an Advance Move:

- **Forwards:** The unit moves forwards a distance up to its Advance Rate. During a forward Advance Move, a unit may perform any number of Wheels.
- **Backwards:** The unit moves backwards a distance up to half its Advance Rate (this is not considered a Characteristic modifier). For example, a unit with Advance Rate 5″ could move backwards 2.5″.
- **Sideways:** The unit moves to either side a distance up to half its Advance Rate (this is not considered a Characteristic modifier).

When performing an Advance Move, no model can end its movement with its centre farther away than its Advance Rate from its starting position. If a model in the unit performed any action during the movement (such as a Sweeping Attack), the distance moved is measured from the model's starting position to the point on the Battlefield where it performed that action and then to its final position.

12.D.c   March Move

When performing a March Move:

- A unit can only move forwards, up to its March Rate.
- A unit may perform any number of Wheels.
- No model can end its movement with its centre farther away than its March Rate from its starting position. If a model in the unit performed any action during the movement (such as a Sweeping Attack), the distance moved is measured from the model's starting position to the point on the Battlefield where it performed that action and then to its final position.

A unit that has Marched cannot shoot in the following Shooting Phase.

12.D.d   Reform

When performing a Reform:

1	Mark the Centre of the unit.
2	Remove the unit from the Battlefield, and then place it back on the Battlefield in any legal formation and facing any direction (following the Unit Spacing rule), with its Centre in the same place as before.

After the Reform, no model can end up with its centre farther away than its March Rate from its starting position. A unit that has Reformed cannot shoot in the following Shooting Phase.

12.D.e Moving Single Model Units

Units consisting of a single model follow the rules for Moving Units stated above. In addition, they can perform any number of Pivots during Advance Moves and March Moves.

12.E Pivots and Wheels

When performing a Pivot:

1	Mark the Centre of the unit.
2	Remove the unit from the Battlefield, and then place it back on the Battlefield facing any direction with its Centre in the same place as before (following the Unit Spacing rule).

When performing a Wheel, rotate the unit forwards up to 90°, around either of its front corners. The distance moved by the unit is equal to the distance the outer front corner of the outermost model in the first rank has moved from its starting to its ending position (not the actual distance it moved along the arc of a circle), see figure 24. All models in the unit are considered to have moved this distance.

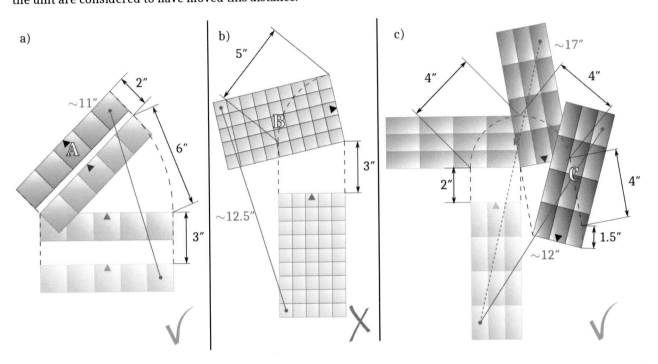

Figure 24: Examples of Wheels.

a) The unit has March Rate 12″. It March Moves forwards 3″, Wheels 6″ (measured from the outer corner from its starting to its ending position), and then March Moves forwards another 2″. The unit has moved 3 + 6 + 2 = 11″.

b) The unit has March Rate 10″. It March Moves forwards 3″ and then performs a 5″ Wheel. Even though the outer corner has only moved 8″, there are models in the unit that end their movement farther away than their March Rate from their starting position, making this move illegal (see "March Move", page 51).

c) The unit has March Rate 16″. It March Moves forwards 2″, then performs 2 Wheels (4″ each), making it almost face the opposite direction. The unit then moves forwards 4″ and finishes the move with a small 1.5″ Wheel. The total distance covered by the unit is 2 + 4 + 4 + 4 + 1.5 = 15.5″.

Even though some models in the unit are temporarily farther from their starting position than their March Rate, this is a legal move, since at the end of the move, all models are within their March Rate of their starting position.

13   Magic Phase

The Magic Phase is when your Wizards will attempt to cast spells, and your opponent can attempt to dispel them.

13.A   Magic Phase Sequence

The Magic Phase is divided into the following steps:

1	Start of the Magic Phase
2	Draw a Flux Card
3	Siphon the Veil
4	Cast a spell with one of your models (see "Spell Casting Sequence", page 57)
5	Repeat step 4 for each spell the Active Player wishes to cast
6	End of the Magic Phase

13.B   Wizards

Models that can cast non-Bound Spells are referred to as Wizards. There are 3 types of Wizards (see "Spell Selection", page 36 and "Model Rules", page 92 for details on the differences between them):

- Wizard Apprentices
- Wizard Adepts (Channel (1))
- Wizard Masters (Channel (1) and a +1 Casting Modifier)

Each of your Wizards has to choose an available Path of Magic to select spells from; the chosen Path of Magic has to be written down on your Army List.

13.C   Magic Dice

In the Magic Phase, spells are cast and dispelled using a pool of dice called the Magic Dice. The number of Magic Dice each player receives in each Magic Phase is determined by which Flux Cards are drawn (see Flux Cards below) and what decisions are made during Siphon the Veil (see "Siphon the Veil", page 54).

13.D   Flux Cards

Each player has a deck consisting of the 8 Flux Cards given in figure 25. During step 2 of the Magic Phase, the Reactive Player randomly draws one of the Flux Cards from the Active Player's deck. This card determines how many starting Magic Dice both players receive in this Magic Phase, and how many Veil Tokens the Active Player receives. Once a Flux Card has been drawn, it is discarded from the deck. The remaining Flux Cards in the decks are open information to both players.

Instead of using Flux Cards, you may use dice to randomise which Flux Card to use. Mark which cards have already been used and roll again whenever you get an already used card. Here is an example of how to randomise using two D6: roll the first dice until its result, called X, is within 1–4. Then roll the second D6. If this D6 rolls 4+, add 4 to X. This will result in a value between 1 and 8.

Flux Card 1	**Flux Card 2**	**Flux Card 3**	**Flux Card 4**
4 Magic Dice (both players)	**5 Magic Dice** (both players)	**5 Magic Dice** (both players)	**5 Magic Dice** (both players)
3 Veil Tokens (Active Player)	**2 Veil Tokens** (Active Player)	**5 Veil Tokens** (Active Player)	**7 Veil Tokens** (Active Player)
All Miscasts this phase gain a **+1** Miscast Modifier			

Flux Card 5	**Flux Card 6**	**Flux Card 7**	**Flux Card 8**
5 Magic Dice (both players)	**6 Magic Dice** (both players)	**6 Magic Dice** (both players)	**7 Magic Dice** (both players)
9 Veil Tokens (Active Player)	**5 Veil Tokens** (Active Player)	**7 Veil Tokens** (Active Player)	**7 Veil Tokens** (Active Player)
			All Miscasts this phase suffer a **−1** Miscast Modifier

Figure 25: Flux Cards.

13.E Siphon the Veil

The Active Player creates a new pool of Veil Tokens that will last until their next Siphon the Veil phase.

- Add the number of Veil Tokens left in their previous Veil Token pool
- Add the number of Veil Tokens given by the Flux Card drawn this Player Turn
- Add Veil Tokens from other sources, such as Channel (see "Channel (X)", page 93)

Up to 12 Veil Tokens can now be removed from the pool to be converted into Magic Dice by the Active Player. For each full 3 Veil Tokens that were removed, the Active Player adds a single Magic Dice to their Magic Dice pool. Up to 4 Magic Dice may be added to the Active Player's pool this way.

13.F Veil Token Limits

At the end of Siphon the Veil, the Active Player must discard Veil Tokens from their Veil Token pool until it contains no more than 3 tokens. The remaining Veil Tokens are saved to be added to the Veil Token pool in the Active Player's next Magic Phase.

Some armies can generate Veil Tokens outside Siphon the Veil. This cannot increase the Veil Token pool beyond 6 Veil Tokens.

13.G Spells

Spells are cast during the Magic Phase. Most spells belong to a specific Path of Magic.

13.G.a   Spell Properties

All spells are defined by the following 6 properties (see figure 26):

1 – Spell Classification	Spells are classified into the different categories Learned Spells, Attribute Spells, and Hereditary Spells by letters or numbers.
2 – Spell Name	Use the spell name to state which spell you intend to cast.
3 – Casting Value	The Casting Value is the minimum value you need to reach to succeed a Casting Attempt. Spells may have different Casting Values available (see "Boosted Spells", page 57).
4 – Type	The spell type describes how the spell's targets have to be chosen.
5 – Duration	The duration of a spell determines how long the effects of the spell are applied.
6 – Effect	The effect of a spell defines what happens to the target of the spell when the spell is successfully cast. Spell effects are never affected by Special Items, Model Rules, other spell effects, or similar abilities affecting the Caster, unless specifically stated otherwise.

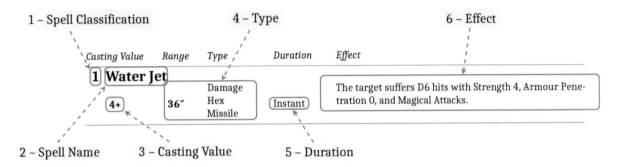

Figure 26: Spell Properties in The 9ᵗʰ Age: Fantasy Battles – Arcane Compendium.

13.G.b   Spell Classification

All spells are part of one or more of the following categories:

13.G.b.1 Learned Spells

All spells labelled with a number are Learned Spells, which are the main spells of a Path. They are usually numbered from 1 to 6, which is relevant for the Spell Selection rules.

Each player may only attempt to cast each Learned Spell once per Magic Phase, even if it is known by different Wizards (unless the spell is Replicable, see below).

13.G.b.2 Hereditary Spells

Most Army Books contain a Hereditary Spell, which is labelled "**H**" instead of a number. Hereditary Spells follow all the rules for Learned Spells.

13.G.b.3 Attribute Spells

Attribute Spells are labelled "**A**". All Wizards that know at least one spell from a Path of Magic automatically know the Attribute Spell from that Path if there is any.

Path Attribute Spells are special spells that cannot be cast independently. Instead, the Caster may cast the Attribute Spell automatically each time it successfully casts a non-Attribute Spell from the corresponding Path. This means that an Attribute Spell can be cast more than once by the same Caster, and also by different Casters during a Magic Phase. Attribute Spells cannot be dispelled.

13.G.b.4 Replicable Spells

Some Learned Spells are Replicable Spells and are labelled "***rep***". The player may attempt to cast Replicable Spells multiple times in the same Magic Phase, but each Wizard may only make a single attempt.

13.G.b.5 Bound Spells

Some spells are classified as Bound Spells, which follow different rules than the above (see "Bound Spells", page 59).

13.G.c Spell Types

The spell type describes which targets can be chosen for the spell. Unless specifically stated otherwise, a spell may only have a single target and the target must be a single unit. If a spell has more than one type, apply all the restrictions of each type.

For example, if a spell has the types Direct, Hex, and Range 12", the target must be in the Caster's Front Arc, be an enemy unit, and be within 12" of the Caster.

Augment	The spell may only target friendly units (or friendly models inside units if Focused).
Aura	This spell has an area of effect. Its effects are applied to all possible targets, according to the rest of the spell types, within X" of the Caster. For example, a spell with Augment, Aura, and Range 12" targets all friendly units within 12" of the Caster.
Caster	The spell targets only the model casting the spell (unless Focused, all model parts are affected).
Caster's Unit	The spell targets only the Caster's unit.
Damage	The spell may only target units and/or models not currently Engaged in Combat.
Direct	The spell may only target units and/or models in the Caster's Front Arc.
Focused	The spell may only target single models (including a Character inside a unit). If the target is a Multipart Model (such as a chariot with riders and pulling beasts, or a knight and its mount), only one model part may be targeted.
Ground	The spell doesn't target units or models. Instead, the target is a point on the Battlefield.
Hex	The spell may only target enemy units (or enemy models inside units if Focused).
Missile	The spell may only target units and/or models within the Caster's Line of Sight. It cannot be cast if the Caster (or its unit) is Engaged in Combat.
Range X"	The spell has a maximum casting range. Only targets within X" can be chosen. This casting range is always indicated in the corresponding column in the spell's profile (see figure 26). Note that any effects that alter a spell's range do not affect any other distance specifications that may be part of the spell's effect.
Universal	The spell may target both friendly and enemy units (or models inside units if Focused).

13.G.d Spell Duration

The spell duration specifies how long the effects of the spell are applied. A spell duration can either be Instant, One Turn, or Permanent as described below:

13.G.d.1 Instant

The effect of the spell has no lasting duration: effects are applied when the spell is cast. Afterwards the spell ends automatically.

13.G.d.2 One Turn

The effect of the spell lasts until the start of the Caster's next Magic Phase. If an affected unit is divided into several units (the most common example being a Character leaving its unit), each of the units formed this way keeps being affected by the spell effects. Characters that join a unit affected by One Turn spells are not affected by these spells, and likewise, units joined by Characters affected by One Turn spells are not affected either.

13.G.d.3 Permanent

The effect of the spell lasts until the end of the game or until a designated ending condition is met (as detailed in the spell effect). The spell can only be removed by the method described in the spell. If an affected unit is divided into several units, follow the same restrictions as for One Turn spells.

13.H   Spell Casting Sequence

Each of the Active Player's non-Fleeing models with one or more spells may now attempt to cast each of its spells up to one time per Magic Phase. The model is referred to as the Caster. In each Magic Phase one Casting Attempt may be made for each spell, even if this spell is known by different Wizards. Remember that Bound Spells, Attribute Spells, and Replicable Spells ignore this restriction.

Each casting of a spell is resolved as follows:

A	Casting Attempt. If failed, skip steps B–F
B	Dispelling Attempt. If successful, skip steps C–F
C	In case of Broken Concentration, skip steps D–E and go directly to step F
D	Resolve the spell effect
E	If applicable, choose target(s) for the Attribute Spell and resolve its effect
F	If applicable, apply the Miscast effect

13.H.a   Casting Attempt

Each Casting Attempt is resolved as follows:

1	The Active Player declares which Wizard is casting which spell and how many Magic Dice will be used. If applicable, they also declare which version of the spell is used and what its targets are. Between 1 and 5 dice from the Active Player's Magic Dice pool must be used.
2	The Active Player rolls the chosen number of Magic Dice from the Magic Dice pool and adds the results of the rolled dice and any Casting Modifiers together (see "Casting and Dispelling Modifiers", page 58). This total is referred to as the total casting roll.
3	The Casting Attempt is passed if the total casting roll is **equal to or greater** than the spell's Casting Value. The Casting Attempt fails if the total casting roll is less than the spell's Casting Value. Note that the Casting Attempt may Fizzle if 2 or more dice were used (see "Fizzle", page 58).

13.H.a.1 Boosted Spells

Some spells have two Casting Values, with the greater Casting Value being referred to as the Boosted version of the spell. Boosted versions may have their type (range, target restrictions) and/or duration modified (e.g. giving the spell a longer range), and/or the effects of the spell changed. Declare if you are trying to cast the Boosted version before rolling any dice. If no declaration is made, the basic version for the chosen target is assumed to be used.

13.H.b   Dispelling Attempt

Whenever the Active Player passes a Casting Attempt, the Reactive Player may attempt to dispel the Casting Attempt:

1	The Reactive Player declares how many Magic Dice will be used from their pool. The Reactive Player must use at least 1 dice for a Dispelling Attempt. Note that there is no maximum number of Magic Dice allowed to be used for a Dispelling Attempt.
2	The Reactive Player rolls the chosen number of dice and adds the results of the rolled dice and any Dispelling Modifiers together (see "Casting and Dispelling Modifiers", page 58), to get the total dispelling roll.
3	The Dispelling Attempt is successful if the total dispelling roll is **equal to or greater** than the total casting roll. If so, the spell is dispelled and the spell is not cast. The Dispelling Attempt fails if the total dispelling roll is less than the total casting roll. If so, the spell is successfully cast. Note that the Dispelling Attempt may Fizzle if 2 or more dice were used (see "Fizzle", page 58).

13.H.c   Resolve the Spell

If the spell was not dispelled, it is successfully cast. Apply the spell effects. Afterwards (if applicable), choose a target for the Path Attribute Spell and immediately apply its effects (Attribute Spells cannot be dispelled).

13.H.d Additional Rules Affecting Casting and Dispelling Attempts

13.H.d.1 Casting and Dispelling Modifiers

There are many potential sources for modifiers to the roll (the most common modifier for casting rolls is the +1 to cast modifier for being a Wizard Master). Add these modifiers to the casting or dispelling rolls. After all modifiers are applied, total Casting and Dispelling Modifiers may not exceed +2 and −2.

13.H.d.2 Fizzle

When a Casting Attempt or Dispelling Attempt is failed for which 2 dice or more were used, any Magic Dice that rolled a natural '1' are returned to the Magic Dice pool they were taken from. Note that this does not apply to passed Casting Attempts that are then dispelled.

13.I Miscasts

When a player rolls their casting roll and three or more Magic Dice roll the same value, the Casting Attempt results in a Miscast (regardless of whether the Casting Attempt is passed or not). If the Casting Attempt is successful and not dispelled, apply the effects of the Miscast, as determined by the value on the Magic Dice as shown in table 4.

If **3 Magic Dice** were used for the casting roll, apply a −1 Miscast Modifier (see "Miscast Modifiers and Miscast Table" below).

If **5 Magic Dice** were used for the casting roll, apply a +1 Miscast Modifier.

13.I.a Miscast Modifiers and Miscast Table

A +X or −X Miscast Modifier means that X is added to or deducted from the value of the dice yielding the Miscast. For example, a 222 Miscast with a +1 Miscast Modifier makes a 222 counts as a 333 Miscast.

Three of a kind:	Miscast Effects Apply the effects of 222 and higher after resolving the effects of the spell and any Attribute Spell
000 or lower	No effect.
111	**Broken Concentration** The Casting Attempt fails (apply Fizzle as normal).
222	**Witchfire** The Caster's unit suffers **1D6 hits** with Armour Penetration 2, Magical Attacks, and a Strength equal to the number of Magic Dice that were used for the casting roll.
333	**Magical Inferno** The Caster's unit suffers **2D6 hits** with Armour Penetration 2, Magical Attacks, and a Strength equal to the number of Magic Dice that were used for the casting roll.
444	**Amnesia** The Caster cannot cast the Miscast spell anymore this game.
555	**Backlash** The Caster suffers **2 hits** that wound on 4+ with Armour Penetration 10 and Magical Attacks.
666	**Implosion** The Caster suffers **4 hits** that wound on 4+ with Armour Penetration 10 and Magical Attacks.
777 or higher	**Breach in the Veil** The Caster's model is removed as a casualty (no saves of any kind allowed).

Table 4: Miscast Table.

13.J Bound Spells

Bound Spells can also be cast by models that are not Wizards, but possessing a Bound Spell does not make a model a Wizard. A Bound Spell is a spell that is usually contained in a magical artefact of some sort. Bound Spells cannot be used to cast Boosted versions of the spell they contain. A Bound Spell containing a spell from a Path with an Attribute also automatically contains the Path Attribute Spell.

13.J.a Power Level

All Bound Spells have two Power Levels, given as values in brackets (usually Power Level (4/8)). The first value is the Bound Spell's primary Power Level. This is used when the Bound Spell is cast with 2 Magic Dice. The second value is the Bound Spell's secondary Power Level, and is used when the Bound Spell is cast with 3 Magic Dice.

13.J.b Casting a Bound Spell

Casting a Bound Spell ignores the normal Casting Attempt rules, and instead follows a different procedure. Each of the Active Player's non-Fleeing models with Bound Spells may attempt to cast each of its Bound Spells up to one time per Magic Phase. This model is referred to as the Caster. Bound Spells can be cast even if the same spell has already been cast earlier in the same Magic Phase. Casting a Bound Spell does not prevent the casting of the same spell later in the same Magic Phase, even as non-Bound Spell.

13.J.b.1 Bound Spell Casting Attempt

1	The Active Player declares which model will cast which Bound Spell, and whether they will use 2 or 3 Magic Dice. If applicable, the Active Player also declares the targets of the spell. The spell is always cast with the basic version as Bound Spells cannot be Boosted.
2	The Active Player removes the chosen number of Magic Dice (2 or 3) from their Magic Dice pool (do not roll them).
3	The Casting Attempt is always passed.

Note that Bound Spells that contain a spell from a Path with an Attribute automatically also contain the Path Attribute Spell, and that unless specifically stated otherwise Casting Modifiers are not applied to the casting roll of a Bound Spell.

13.J.b.2 Bound Spell Dispelling Attempt

Dispelling a Bound Spell works exactly like dispelling a Learned Spell. If 2 Magic Dice were removed the casting roll is equal to the Bound Spell's primary Power Level. If 3 Magic Dice were removed the casting roll is equal to the Bound Spell's secondary Power Level.

13.K Magical Effects

13.K.a Magical Move

Some spells or abilities enable a unit to perform a Magical Move. The move is performed as if in step 3 of the Movement Phase Sequence (Moving Units), which means that it follows the same rules and restrictions as if this was a new Moving Units sub-phase (e.g. Fleeing units, Shaken units, units with Random Movement, or units Engaged in Combat cannot move). Actions that a unit could normally do in the Moving Units sub-phase can be made (such as Wheeling, Reforming, joining units, leaving units, and so on).

A Magical Move always has a limited movement range (e.g. "the target may perform a 12″ Magical Move"): the target's Advance Rate and March Rate are **always** equal to this value for the duration of the move. A unit can only perform a single Magical Move per Magic Phase.

13.K.b   Recover Health Points

Some spells or abilities can recover Health Points lost earlier in the battle. The amount of Health Points recovered is noted in the ability (Recover X Health Points). Recovering Health Points can never bring back models that have been removed as casualties, and cannot increase a model's Health Points above its starting value.

A Character inside a Combined Unit never recovers Health Points from abilities that allow a unit to recover Health Points. A Character can only recover Health Points when it is the only target of an ability or spell.

Any excess Recovered Health Points are lost.

13.K.c   Raise Health Points

Raise Health Points uses the rules for Recover Health Points with the exception that Raise Health Points can bring back models that have been removed as casualties. Bringing back models is subject to the following rules and restrictions:

- First, recover all lost Health Points on models in the unit (except for Characters), then bring back models in the following order: first Champions, then other R&F models (including Musicians and Standard Bearers). Each Raised model must be recovered to its full amount of Health Points before another model can be Raised. This cannot Raise a unit's number of models above its starting number. Any excess Raised Health Points are lost.

- Raised models without Front Rank must be placed in the rear rank if incomplete, or in a new rear rank if the current rear rank is complete. In units with one rank (including single model units), a Raised model can either be placed in the first rank or you can declare the first rank complete and create a new rank. Any models that cannot be placed in legal positions are lost.

- Any used One use only effects, or destroyed equipment (Special Items or mundane equipment) are not regained.

- Raised models are subject to the same ongoing effects as their unit, and count as Charging if their unit Charged.

13.K.d   Summoned Units

Summoned units are units created during the game. All models in a newly Summoned unit must be deployed within the range of the ability. If the unit is summoned as a result of a Ground type spell, at least one of the Summoned models must be placed on the targeted point and all models must be within the spell's range. Summoned models must be placed at least 1″ away from other units and from Impassable Terrain. If the whole unit cannot be deployed, then no models can be deployed. Once Summoned, the newly created unit operates as a normal unit on the Caster's side. Summoned units do not award Victory Points to the opponent when they are destroyed.

14   Shooting Phase

In the Shooting Phase, models with Shooting Attacks get a chance to use them.

14.A   Shooting Phase Sequence

The Shooting Phase is divided into the following steps.

1	Start of the Shooting Phase
2	Select one of your units and perform a Shooting Attack
3	Repeat step 2 with a different unit that has not performed a Shooting Attack during this phase yet
4	When all units that can (and want to) shoot have done so, the Shooting Phase ends

14.A.a   Shooting With a Unit

Some units have Shooting Weapons or Model Rules that allow them to perform Shooting Attacks. Apply the following rules for shooting with a unit:

1. Choose a shooting unit

Each unit that can perform a Shooting Attack can do so once per Shooting Phase, with the following conditions and restrictions:

- Fleeing units, Shaken units, units that are Engaged in Combat or were Engaged in Combat at any point during the Player Turn, and units that have Marched or Reformed this Player Turn cannot perform Shooting Attacks.

- All models in the same unit must shoot at the same target, and **only models in the first and second rank may shoot**.

- If models in the unit have more than one type of Shooting Attack, declare which one is used. All R&F models except Champions must use the same type. Champions and Characters are free to use other types of Shooting Attacks (still maximum one attack per model, and directed at the same target as the unit).

- In case of Multipart Models, each model part can make a Shooting Attack in the same phase.

2. Choose a target

Nominate an enemy unit within the shooting unit's Line of Sight as target. Units Engaged in Combat cannot be chosen as targets.

3. Choose models to shoot with

Now determine which models from the shooting unit will shoot at the target unit:

- Check the Line of Sight for each shooting model. Remember that Line of Sight is always drawn from the model's Front Facing. Models that do not have Line of Sight to at least one model in the target unit cannot shoot.

- Measure the range to the target unit for each individual shooting model. This is measured from the actual position of each shooting model to the closest point of the target's Unit Boundary (even if this particular point is not within Line of Sight). Models that are further away from their target than the range of their weapon cannot shoot (unless performing a Stand and Shoot Charge Reaction).

- If the Shooting Attack has a minimum range, the model can only shoot if the target is at least partially outside the minimum range.

- Any model part in the unit is free to choose not to shoot.

4. Shoot!

Once you have established which models will shoot, these models shoot as many times as indicated in their weapon's profile. For each shot, roll to hit with each model, as described below, and then follow the Attack Sequence rules (page 19) after determining the number of hits.

14.B Aim

A Shooting Weapon's Aim tells you what the model needs to roll on a D6 to successfully hit its target. This roll is called a **to-hit roll**. A weapon's Aim is written in brackets after the weapon's name. Each unit has its own Aim for a given Shooting Weapon available to it. For example, an elven archer might have a Longbow (3+) while a human peasant only has a Longbow (4+). The elf would hit its target if it rolls 3 or higher on a D6, while the human would need to roll 4 or higher.

14.C To-Hit Modifiers

Shooting Attacks may suffer one or more to-hit modifiers to their to-hit rolls. If so, simply modify the dice roll for the shot with the given modifiers. The most common to-hit modifiers are explained below and summarised in table 5. If one or more hits are scored, follow the procedure described under "Attacks", page 18. A natural roll of '1' is always a miss.

Long Range	−1	Stand and Shoot	−1
(if Accurate)	0	Soft Cover	−1
Moving and Shooting	−1	Hard Cover	−2
(if Quick to Fire)	0	Hard Target (X)	−X
(if Unwieldy)	−2		
(if both)	−1		

Table 5: Summary of To-Hit Modifiers.

14.C.a Long Range (−1 to hit)

If the distance from the shooting model to the target is more than half the weapon's range, the shooting model suffers a −1 to-hit modifier. Remember that you measure range for each shooting model individually.

For rules purposes, any model not shooting at Long Range is considered to be at Short Range.

14.C.b Moving and Shooting (−1 to hit)

A model that has moved during this Player Turn suffers a −1 to-hit modifier.

14.C.c Stand and Shoot Charge Reaction (−1 to hit)

Shooting Attacks made as part of a Stand and Shoot Charge Reaction suffer a −1 to-hit modifier.

14.C.d Cover

Cover is determined individually for each shooting model. There are two types of Cover: Soft Cover and Hard Cover. The most common reason for applying Cover is the target being obscured by Terrain or other models, or the target being inside a Terrain Feature.

Determine if the target benefits from Cover as follows:

1	Determine which Arc of the target the shooting model is Located in. The corresponding Facing is referred to as Target Facing.
2	Choose any point on the shooting model's Front Facing.
3	For targets on rectangular bases: • From the chosen point, check how large the fraction of the Target Facing is that is behind obstructions (see figures 28 and 29). • If half or more of the Target Facing is obscured, the target benefits from Cover. For targets on round bases: • From the chosen point, check whether the nearest point on the Target Facing, referred to as Target Point, is behind obstructions. • If this point is obscured, the target benefits from Cover.

Note that:

- This is not Line of Sight. Check what is behind obstructions even outside of the shooting model's Front Arc.

- Models always ignore their own unit and the Terrain Feature they are inside for Cover purposes (e.g. a model shooting from a Forest doesn't suffer a Soft Cover modifier for shooting through or at a target inside that Forest).

14.C.d.1 Target Benefiting from Soft Cover (−1 to hit)

A model shooting at a target that benefits from Soft Cover suffers a − 1 to-hit modifier. Soft Cover applies if more than half of the Target Facing or the Target Point is obscured by either:

- Covering Terrain that contributes to Soft Cover

- Models that **do not** block Line of Sight, except if the target and/or the shooting model is of Gigantic Height (see "Model Classification", page 87), and the obscuring model is of Standard Height (in which case no cover is applied) (remember that Skirmisher and Tall affect what blocks Line of Sight)

For examples, see figure 27 for Cover inside Terrain, and figure 30 for Cover behind intervening models.

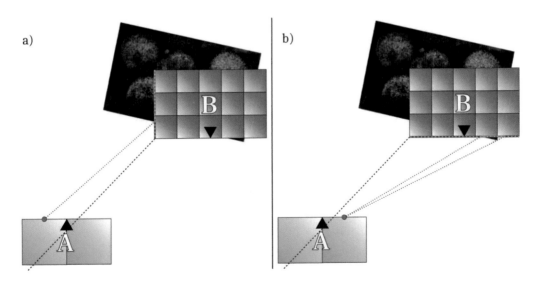

Figure 27: Example of Soft Cover inside a Terrain Feature.

a) The left model in unit A is Located in unit B's Flank Arc, so unit B's Flank Facing is the Target Facing. More than half of the Target Facing is obscured inside the Forest, so unit B benefits from Soft Cover against the left model.

b) The right model in unit A is Located in unit B's Front Arc, so unit B's Front Facing is the Target Facing. Less than half of the Target Facing is obscured inside the Forest, so unit B does not benefit from Soft Cover against the right model.

14.C.d.2 Target Benefiting from Hard Cover (–2 to hit)

A model shooting at a target that benefits from Hard Cover suffers a –2 to-hit modifier. Hard Cover applies if more than half of the Target Facing or the Target Point is obscured by either:

- Covering Terrain that contributes to Hard Cover
- Models that **do** block Line of Sight (remember that Skirmisher and Tall affect what blocks Line of Sight)

See figure 28 for an example of Hard Cover.

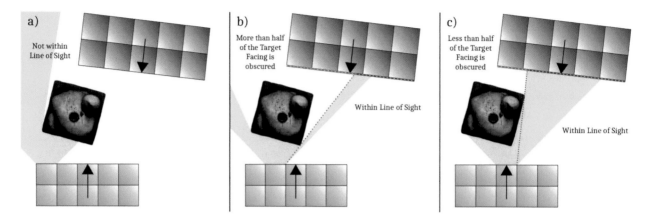

Figure 28: Example of Hard Cover.

a) The model cannot shoot (as its Line of Sight is blocked).

b) The model can shoot (as the enemy is within Line of Sight). Hard Cover is applied since more than half of the Target Facing is obscured by a Terrain Feature that contributes to Hard Cover.

c) The model can shoot (enemy within Line of Sight). No Cover is applied since half or less of the Target Facing is obscured by a Terrain Feature that contributes to Hard Cover.

14.C.d.3 Target Benefiting from Soft and Hard Cover

If a target benefits from both Soft and Hard Cover, only apply the Hard Cover modifier.

If parts of the Target Facing are obscured by obstructions that contribute to Soft and Hard Cover, but not enough to grant either Soft Cover or Hard Cover, apply only the Soft Cover modifier if more than half of the Target Facing is obscured. For example, if 30% of the Target Facing is obscured by Terrain contributing to Soft Cover, and another 30% by Terrain contributing to Hard Cover, then apply the Soft Cover modifier, as 60% of the Target Facing is obscured in total (see figure 29).

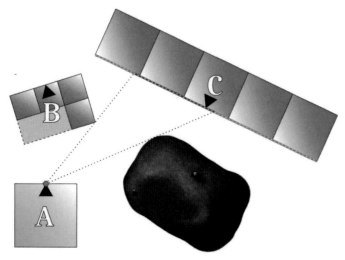

Figure 29: Example of Soft and Hard Cover.

Less than half of the Target Facing is obscured by obstructions contributing either to Soft or Hard Cover. However, more than half is obscured by the combination of both. In this case, the target counts as benefiting from Soft Cover.

14.D   Hopeless Shots

When to-hit modifiers make the needed roll to hit with a Shooting Attack 7+, apply the following procedure:

1	Roll to hit. Rolls of '6' are considered successful.
2	For each successful roll, roll to hit again: on a roll of 4+, this second to-hit roll is successful, and the shot hits.
3	Proceed as described under "Attacks", page 18.

If there are enough modifiers to make the needed roll to hit 8 or more, the shot cannot hit.

For example, a model with Bow (4+) shoots at a target benefiting from Hard Cover (–2 to hit), and is Moving and Shooting (–1). This would require the shooter to roll 7+ on a D6, which means that this shot follows the Hopeless Shots rule. If a '6' is rolled, roll to-hit again. If the shooter manages to roll 4+ on the second attempt, the shot hits.

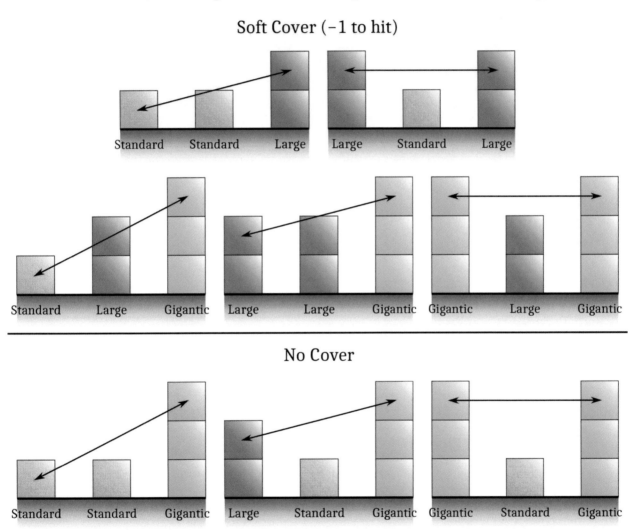

Figure 30: Soft Cover from intervening models.

This diagram shows all possible Height combinations between shooting, target, and intervening models that result in Soft Cover or No Cover. The intervening model is assumed to be placed in such a way that it is sufficiently obscuring the target from the shooter. All other Height combinations yield either Hard Cover or no Line of Sight, depending on whether the target is completely obscured by the intervening model or not.

15   Melee Phase

In the Melee Phase, both players' units Engaged in Combat must attack.

15.A   Melee Phase Sequence

Each Melee Phase is divided into the following steps:

1	Start of the Melee Phase
2	Apply any instances of No Longer Engaged
3	The Active Player chooses a combat that has not already been fought during this Melee Phase
4	Fight a Round of Combat (see "Round of Combat Sequence", page 67)
5	Repeat steps 2–4
6	Once all units that were Engaged in Combat at the start of the phase have fought, the Melee Phase ends

Complete all actions in the Round of Combat Sequence for each unit Engaged in the chosen combat before resolving the next combat.

15.B   Combat

A combat is defined as a group of opposing units that are all connected through base contact. Normally, this would be two units pitted against one another, but it could also be several units against a single enemy unit or a long chain of units from both sides.

15.B.a   First Round of Combat

Certain rules only apply to the First Round of Combat. A unit's First Round of Combat is:

- The Round of Combat after it successfully Charged an enemy unit
- The Round of Combat after it was successfully Charged by an enemy unit if previously unengaged

15.C   No Longer Engaged

Sometimes a unit that was previously Engaged in Combat had all of its opponents removed since the end of the previous Melee Phase. Such units follow the rules described in "No More Foes", page 72. If the unit has not moved since the enemy units were removed (e.g. with a Magical Move), it may perform a Post-Combat Pivot or a Post-Combat Reform, or an Overrun if it just Charged.

15.D   Round of Combat Sequence

Each Round of Combat is divided into the following steps:

1	Start of the Round of Combat
2	Choose a weapon (see "Close Combat Weapons", page 106)
3	Make Way (see "Character", page 102)
4	Issue and accept Duels (see "Duels", page 69)
5	Determine the Initiative Order
6	Roll Melee Attacks, starting with the first Initiative Step: 1. Allocate attacks 2. Roll to hit, to wound, saves, and remove casualties 3. Repeat 1. and 2. for the next Initative Step
7	Calculate which side wins the Round of Combat. Losers roll Break Tests
8	Roll Panic Tests for units within 6″ of friendly Broken units
9	Decide to Restrain or to Pursue
10	Roll Flee Distances
11	Roll Pursuit Distances
12	Move Fleeing units
13	Move Pursuing units
14	Post-Combat Pivots and Post-Combat Reforms
15	Combat Reforms
16	End of the Round of Combat. Proceed to the next combat

15.D.a   Initiative Order

Melee Attacks are performed in Rounds of Combat during the Melee Phase. All Melee Attacks have a specific Agility value that corresponds to the Agility of their model part, unless specifically stated otherwise (such as Impact Hits or Crush Attacks).

Each Round of Combat is fought in a strict striking order, referred to as Initiative Order. The Initiative Order in a combat is determined immediately before any attacks are made. Take into account all modifiers that affect the Agility of attacks that may be performed in this Round of Combat. Once the Initiative Order has been determined for a Round of Combat, it cannot be changed by effects that alter the Agility of attacks during that Round of Combat. The order starts at Initiative Step 10 with all attacks with Agility 10, and is resolved downwards to Initiative Step 0 with all attacks with Agility 0.

At each Initiative Step, all attacks from this step that meet the necessary requirements (see Which Models can Attack, below) strike simultaneously.

15.D.b   Charging Momentum

Charging models gain +1 Agility.

15.D.c   Which Models can Attack

Models in base contact with an enemy attack during their Initiative Step (remember that models are considered to be in base contact across gaps: see "Base Contact between Models across Gaps", page 10). Models from both sides attack in each player's Melee Phase.

15.D.c.1 Supporting Attacks

Models in the second rank and not in base contact with any enemy models can perform Close Combat Attacks across models in the first rank directly in front of them. These Close Combat Attacks are called Supporting Attacks. A model part that performs Supporting Attacks **always** has a maximum Attack Value of X, where X is defined by the Height of the model (see "Model Classification", page 87).

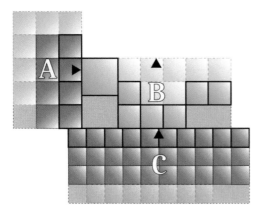

Figure 31: Which models can attack?

Models colour-coded with a darker shade can all strike. Models with a bold frame count as being in base contact with an enemy; note that models are considered to be in base contact across gaps. Models colour-coded with a lighter shade cannot make Supporting Attacks.

Unit C is in Line Formation and thus both the second and third rank can make Supporting Attacks. Unit B is not Engaged in its Front Facing; its models cannot make Supporting Attacks to their Flank or Rear; they could only strike across the first rank.

15.D.d   Allocating Attacks

At each Initiative Step, before any attacks are rolled, Close Combat Attacks must first be allocated towards enemy models. If a model is in base contact with more than one enemy model, it can choose which model to attack. Attacks can be allocated towards models with different Health Pools, i.e. R&F models, Champions, and Characters (see "Attacks", page 18). The number of Close Combat Attacks a model can make is equal to its Attack Value, which can be modified by equipment, Attack Attributes, spells, etc. If a model has an Attack Value above 1, it can allocate its Close Combat Attacks towards different enemy models in base contact. If a model is making Supporting Attacks, it can allocate its attacks as if it was in the first rank of the unit (in the same file). Allocate all attacks at each Initiative Step before making any to-hit rolls.

15.D.d.1   Swirling Melee

R&F models Engaged in Combat may be in positions in the unit where, based on the general rules for allocating attacks, they can either:

- allocate attacks (including Supporting Attacks) only towards enemy Characters or Champions
- not allocate any attacks at all due to enemy models fighting a Duel

Such models may elect to allocate their Close Combat Attacks towards R&F models of the same unit instead. Note that Swirling Melee cannot be used by Characters.

Figure 32 illustrates how attacks can be allocated in a complex case.

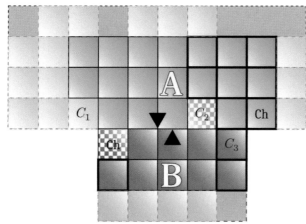

Figure 32: Example for allocating attacks.

The Champion of unit B (Ch) and Character C_2 are locked in a Duel (indicated by the chess pattern). This means that they can only allocate attacks towards each other. The magenta and green models can allocate attacks towards the R&F models of the other unit. The models with a bold frame can allocate attacks towards Characters/Champions. The models in fainter colours with dashed frames cannot attack at all. Character C_1 cannot attack because the only model it is in base contact with is a Champion that is locked in a Duel. If C_1 was a R&F model, it could allocate attacks towards the magenta R&F models.

15.D.e Rolling to Hit

Roll a D6 for each Close Combat Attack, referred to as to-hit rolls. The needed roll to hit the target is determined by the difference between the Offensive Skill of the attacking model part and the Defensive Skill of the model the attack was allocated towards. See table 6 below.

To-hit modifiers can alter this to-hit roll. Close Combat to-hit rolls that are modified to hit on better than 2+ always fail on a natural roll of '1', while they are always successful on a natural roll of '6' even if they are modified beyond 6+.

Example: a model has Offensive Skill 3, Attack Value 2, and is equipped with Paired Weapons, which gives it a total of 3 attacks. The model may allocate two attacks towards a model with Defensive Skill 2, which hit on 3+, and one towards a model with Defensive Skill 8, which hits on 5+.

Once you have determined the number of hits, follow the Attack Sequence rules (page 19).

Offensive Skill minus Defensive Skill	Needed roll to hit
4 or more	2+
1 to 3	3+
0 to −3	4+
−4 to −7	5+
−8 or less	6+

Table 6: Close Combat to-Hit Table.

15.D.f Losing Base Contact

Removing casualties may cause units to lose base contact with their foe. When this happens, units are nudged back into combat using the following procedure:

1. The unit that is going to lose base contact while not suffering casualties is moved the minimum amount needed to keep the units in base contact.

2. If this will not bring the units back into contact, move the unit suffering casualties the minimum amount needed to keep the units in base contact.

A nudged unit can only be moved in a straight line forwards, backwards, to either side, or a combination of two of these directions (first one, then the other). Units that are in base contact with other enemy units can never be nudged in this way. Nudged units cannot move through the Unit Boundary of other units or Impassable Terrain. They also cannot move into base contact with enemy units that they were not in base contact with before the nudge move, but they are allowed to move within 1″ of the Unit Boundary of other units Engaged in the same Combat. Nudge moves cannot be used to change the Facing in which any unit is fighting (which means that if the unit was Engaged in the Flank before the nudge move, this must still be true after the nudge move). If several units lose base contact at the same time, move them in the order that allows the maximum number of units to stay in combat. If this number is equal, the Active Player decides the order.

If nudging either unit does not manage to bring the units back into contact with each other, the unit Drops out of Combat. Any units that are no longer Engaged in Combat follow the rules given under "No More Foes", page 72.

15.E Duels

15.E.a Issuing a Duel

Characters and Champions Engaged in Combat may issue a Duel at step 4 of the Round of Combat Sequence (see "Round of Combat Sequence", page 67). The Active Player may nominate one of their Characters or Champions and issue a Duel, provided that there is at least one enemy Champion or Character able to accept it (this enemy model's unit must be in base contact with the unit of the model that issued the Duel, and there must not be any ongoing Duel in this combat; see below).

If the Duel was refused, or if no Duel was issued, the Reactive Player may nominate one of their Characters or Champions that did not refuse the Active Player's Duel and issue a Duel.

15.E.b Accepting or Refusing a Duel

If a Duel was issued, the opponent may now choose one of their own Characters or Champions Engaged in the same Combat to accept the Duel and fight the Character or Champion that issued the Duel. The model that accepts the Duel must be in a unit that is in base contact with the unit of the model that issued the Duel.

If a Duel isn't accepted it is said to be refused. The player issuing the Duel now nominates one of their opponent's Characters that could have accepted the Duel, if there is any (note that Champions cannot be nominated).

The chosen model:

- Has its Discipline **set** to 0, and it loses Stubborn (if it has it)
- Cannot perform any Melee Attacks
- Loses Rally Around the Flag (if it has it)
- In case of a Battle Standard Bearer, doesn't add +1 to its side's Combat Score

The effects end:

- At the end of the Player Turn in which the combat ends
- When the chosen Character accepts or issues a Duel
- At the end of the Player Turn if there no longer is an enemy model Engaged in the same Combat that could accept a Duel

15.E.c Fighting a Duel

If the Duel was accepted, the model that issued the Duel and the model that accepted the Duel will fight the Duel based on the following rules:

- The two models count as being in base contact with each other (even if their bases are not physically touching each other) and must allocate all their Close Combat Attacks towards each other.
- Melee Attacks made towards a unit as a whole (such as Breath Attacks, Impact Hits, Grind Attacks, Stomp Attacks) can only be distributed onto the opposing duellist. Melee Attacks made at specific models (such as all models in base contact) are unaffected and work as normal.
- No other model can allocate attacks towards either of these models, and attacks/hits from Melee Attacks can never be distributed onto a model that is fighting a Duel.
- If one of the models is removed as a casualty in the Melee Phase before the other model had a chance to make all its Melee Attacks (this is a common situation with Characters that have attacks with more than one Agility value, such as a rider and its mount, or a model with Stomp Attacks), any of the attacks not yet carried out can and must be directed at the removed model, as if it was still Engaged and in base contact, in order to get an Overkill bonus. Note that the gap from the removed model is filled immediately during the Initiative Step in which the model is removed, according to the rules for "Removing Champions and Characters", page 81.
- If one of the models is removed as a casualty, Breaks, or if the combat ends for any reason (including being divided through Splitting Combat), the Duel ends at the end of the phase. If neither model is removed as a casualty and both their units are still Engaged with one another at the beginning of the next Round of Combat, the Duel continues. No other Duel can be issued in the same combat before the Duel ends.

15.E.d Overkill

During a Duel, any excess Health Point losses caused count towards the Combat Score, up to a maximum of +3.

15.F Winning a Round of Combat

15.F.a Combat Score

Once all Initiative Steps have passed (i.e. all models have had a chance to attack), the winner of this Round of Combat is determined by calculating each side's Combat Score. Simply add up all Combat Score bonuses. The side with the higher Combat Score wins the Round of Combat and the side with the lower Combat Score loses the Round of Combat. If there is a tie, both sides are treated as winners. The different Combat Score bonuses are described below and summarised in table 7.

15.F.a.1 Lost Health Points on enemy units: +1 for each Health Point

Each player adds up the number of Health Points lost from their opponent's units (Engaged in the same Combat) during this Round of Combat. This includes enemies that were Engaged in the Combat but Dropped out of Combat or were completely wiped out during this Round of Combat.

15.F.a.2 Overkill: +1 for each Health Point (maximum +3)

In a Duel, excess Health Points lost by the enemy model after it was removed as a casualty are counted towards the Combat Score. A maximum of +3 can be added to your Combat Score due to Overkill. Note that excess Health Point losses are only counted when fighting a Duel. In all other situations, excess Health Point losses count for nothing.

15.F.a.3 Charge: +1

Each side with one or more Charging models receives +1 to their Combat Score.

15.F.a.4 Rank Bonus: +1 for each Full Rank after the first (maximum +3)

Each side adds +1 to their Combat Score for each Full Rank after the first in a single unit, up to a maximum of +3. Only count this for a single unit per side (use the unit that gives the highest Rank Bonus). Units in Line Formation cannot add Rank Bonus to their Combat Score.

15.F.a.5 Standards: +1 for each Standard and Battle Standard Bearer

Each side adds +1 to their Combat Score for each Standard Bearer and Battle Standard Bearer Engaged in Combat at the end of the Round of Combat.

15.F.a.6 Flank Bonus: +1 or +2

Each side adds +1 to their Combat Score if they have one or more units fighting an enemy in the enemy's Flank. If at least one of these units (that are fighting an enemy in its Flank) has one or more Full Ranks, add +2 instead.

15.F.a.7 Rear Bonus: +2 or +3

Each side adds +2 to their Combat Score if they have one or more units fighting an enemy in the enemy's Rear. If at least one of these units (that are fighting an enemy in its Rear) has one or more Full Ranks, add +3 instead.

15.F.a.8 Combat Score Summary

Health Points Lost by Enemy Units	+1 for each Health Point
Overkill	+1 for each Health Point (maximum +3)
Charge	+1
Rank Bonus	+1 for each Full Rank after the first (maximum +3)
Standard	+1 for each Standard and Battle Standard Bearer
Flank Bonus	+1 or +2
Rear Bonus	+2 or +3

Table 7: Combat Score Summary.

15.G   Break Test

Each unit on the side that lost the Round of Combat must take a Break Test. The order is chosen by the losing player. A Break Test is a Discipline Test with a negative modifier equal to the Combat Score difference (i.e. if the Combat Score was 6 to 3, the units on the losing side take Break Tests with a −3 modifier).

If the test is passed, the unit remains Engaged in the Combat. If the test is failed, the unit Breaks and Flees. Remember that units within 6" of a friendly unit that Breaks must take a Panic Test (see Panic Test).

15.G.a   Steadfast

Any units that have more Full Ranks than each of the enemy units Engaged in the same Combat are considered Steadfast. Steadfast units ignore Discipline modifiers from the Combat Score difference when rolling Break Tests (and tests to Combat Reform).

15.G.b   Disrupted Ranks

A unit cannot use the Steadfast rule if it is Engaged in Combat in its Flank or Rear with an enemy unit with at least 2 Full Ranks.

15.G.c   No More Foes

Sometimes a unit destroys all enemy units in base contact and finds itself no longer Engaged in Combat (so it cannot provide Combat Score bonuses such as Standards or Flank). These units always count as winning the combat, and can either make an Overrun (if they were Charging), a Post-Combat Pivot, or a Post-Combat Reform.

When this happens in multiple combats, the Combat Score resulting from lost Health Points by the unit and its enemies counts, but all other Combat Score bonuses are ignored. Note that the unit itself doesn't take a Break Test since it always counts as if on the winning side.

15.G.d   Splitting Combat

If due to removing casualties, two or more disconnected subgroups of opposing units are created (see figure 33), resolve the Combat normally (accounting for every unit that took part in this Round of Combat), checking any remaining base contact for the purpose of Rear and Flank Bonuses. In the next Melee Phase, each subgroup will be treated as a separate combat.

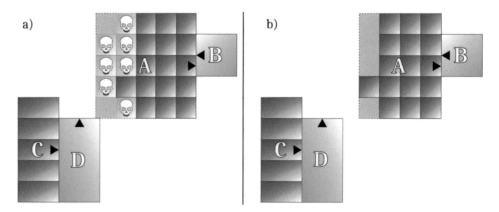

Figure 33: Splitting combat.

a) Unit A suffers casualties, which results in unit D no longer being in base contact. Neither unit A nor unit D can be nudged back into base contact since they are in base contact with other enemies (see "Losing Base Contact", page 69). Calculate Combat Score in this case as one single combat (only unit C grants a Flank Bonus).

b) In the next Player Turn, this situation will count as two separate combats.

15.H   Pursuits and Overruns

Before moving Broken units, each unit that is in base contact with the Broken unit(s) may declare a Pursuit of a single Broken unit (each Pursuing unit may choose any eligible enemy unit to Pursue). Determine the direction of the Flee Move as follows:

- If the Broken unit is in contact with a single enemy unit, its Flee Move will be directed away from that unit.
- If the Broken unit is in contact with more than one enemy unit, the owner of the enemy units must declare which of those units the Flee Move will be directed away from.

To be able to Pursue a Broken enemy, the unit cannot be Engaged with any non-Broken enemy units and must be in base contact with the Broken unit. Units can elect not to Pursue, but must then pass a Discipline Test to succeed in restraining themselves, referred to as Restrain Pursuit Test; if the test is failed, the unit must Pursue anyway. If the test is passed, the unit may do either a Post-Combat Pivot or a Post-Combat Reform.

15.H.1 Overrun

A unit that fought its First Round of Combat after Charging can choose to make a special Pursuit Move called Overrun (instead of a Post-Combat Pivot or Post-Combat Reform), if all enemy units in base contact were wiped out (including units removed from play as a result of Unstable or something similar). Overruns follow the rules for moving Pursuing units, except that step 1. Pivot is ignored (i.e. Overruns are straight forward) and that no Restrain Pursuit Test is required. Check which Arc the Overrunning unit is Located in for each enemy unit that may be Charged later in this process. If the Overrun Move will lead to a Charge, it will be in the Facing determined at this point.

15.H.a   Roll for Flee and Pursuit Distances

Each Broken unit now rolls 2D6 to determine its Flee Distance, and each unit that has declared a Pursuit now rolls 2D6 to determine its Pursuit Distance. If any Pursuing unit rolls a Pursuit Distance **equal or higher** than the Flee Distance of the unit it is Pursuing, the Fleeing unit is immediately destroyed. Remove that unit as a casualty (with no saves of any kind allowed). If several units are Fleeing from the same combat, the units move in the same order as their Flee Distance was rolled (the owner chooses in which order they roll the Flee Distance). The Active Player chooses which player will roll for their Pursuing units first. Each player chooses the order in which they roll the Pursuit Distances of their own Pursuing units.

15.H.b   Flee Distance and Fleeing Units

Each Broken unit that was not captured and destroyed will now Flee directly away from the previously determined enemy unit. Pivot the Fleeing unit so that its Rear Facing is parallel with the Facing it was Engaged in (of the enemy unit the Flee Move is directed away from), and then move the Fleeing unit straight forward a number of inches equal to the Flee Distance rolled earlier. Use the rules for Flee Moves with the exception that units that are Engaged in the same Combat do not cause Dangerous Terrain Tests. If the direction of the Flee Move cannot be determined, e.g. because the enemy units that won the Round of Combat were removed as casualties, the Broken unit Flees directly away from the closest enemy unit instead (Centre of Unit to Centre of Unit).

15.H.c   Pursuit Distance and Pursuing Units

Each Pursuing unit now performs a Pursuit Move, which is divided into three consecutive steps.

Impassable Terrain, enemy units that Fled from the combat involving the Pursuing unit, and friendly units that were not part of that combat are considered to be obstructions for the Pursuit Move. Models cannot move into or through obstructions during Pursuit Moves. All friendly units that were part of the same combat are treated as Open Terrain for steps 1 and 2 of the Pursuit Move.

Before moving any unit, check:

- Which Pursuing unit would Charge an enemy unit (see 2.2 Enemy Unit below). Ignore other Pursuing units potentially rendering the Charge impossible.
- Which Arc the Pursuing unit is Located in for each enemy unit that may be Charged later in this process. If the Pursuit Move will lead to a Charge, it will be in the Facing determined at this point.

The Charging units will be moved first, in the order that best satisfies the priority order of "Maximising Contact", page 42 (see figure 35). Afterwards the remaining Pursuing units will be moved, in an order chosen by the owner.

1. Pivot

The Pursuing unit Pivots so that it is facing the same direction as the Pursued unit, or if destroyed, the direction the Pursued unit would have had, had it not been destroyed. Ignore the Unit Spacing rule during this Pivot.

After the Pivot, one of the four situations below will arise. If more than one is applicable, apply the uppermost one.

1. If the Front Facing of the Pursuing unit would overlap the Board Edge, the unit Pursues off the Board (see "Pursuing off the Board", page 78).

2. If the Front Facing of the Pursuing unit would overlap the Unit Boundary of an enemy unit that did not Flee from the same combat, it declares a Charge against that unit. If there is more than one possible target, the Pivoting unit chooses which to Charge. The Charged unit may not perform any Charge Reactions (not even if already Fleeing). Remove the Pursuing unit from the Battlefield and then place it back on the Battlefield with its Front Facing in base contact with its target, in the Facing determined before the Pivot, maximising the number of Engaged models as normal but keeping the Centre of the unit as close as possible to its starting position while doing so. If there is not enough room to place the Pursuing unit, treat the enemy unit as obstruction instead.

3. If the Front Facing of the Pursuing unit would overlap an obstruction, the unit instead Pivots so that it faces as close as possible towards the direction of the the Pursued unit, while following the Unit Spacing rule (normally this means stopping 1″ away from the obstacle), and then moves no farther (i.e. ignore steps 2 and 3).

4. If the Front Facing of the Pursuing unit touches neither of the above, proceed to step 2. Note that only the Front Facing needs to be clear: Unit Boundaries, Impassable Terrain, or the Board Edge overlapping other parts of the unit are ignored during steps 1–3.

2. Forward Ahead

Without moving the Pursuing unit, check what the first obstacle (Board Edge, enemy Unit Boundary, or obstruction) within the rectangle directly ahead of the unit formed by its Front Facing and the rolled Pursuit Distance would be. The Unit Spacing rule is ignored when doing this check and for all movement during Forward Ahead. If more than one is applicable, apply the uppermost one.

2.1. Board Edge

If the first obstacle would be the Board Edge, move the unit straight forward until it touches the Board Edge and then follow the rules for Pursuing off the Board.

2.2. Enemy Unit

If the first obstacle would be the Unit Boundary of an enemy unit that did not Flee from the same combat, the Pursuing unit declares a Charge against that unit, using its Pursuit Distance roll as its Charge Range. If there is more than one possible target, the Pursuing unit chooses which to Charge. The Charged unit may not perform any Charge Reactions (not even if already Fleeing). The Pursuing unit immediately performs a Charge Move (following all the normal Move Chargers rules) towards the previously determined Facing.

If the Pursuing unit joins a combat that has already been fought or was created during this Melee Phase, it will be resolved in the next Melee Phase (with the Charging unit still counting as Charging). If the Pursuing unit joins a combat that wasn't created during this Melee Phase and that hasn't been fought yet, the unit will have a chance to fight and Pursue again this phase.

If the Charge is not possible to complete, the unit does not perform a Failed Charge Move but treats the enemy unit as obstruction and proceeds to 2.3 instead.

2.3. Obstruction or No Obstacle

If the first obstacle, if any, would not be an enemy Unit Boundary or the Board Edge, the Pursuing unit now moves its Pursuit Distance straight forward. If this brings the Front Facing of the unit into base contact with an obstruction, the unit stops.

3. Legal Position?

At the end of the Pursuit Move, check if the unit is in a legal position. It cannot be in base contact with a unit it didn't declare a Charge against, and it must follow the Unit Spacing rule, which includes friendly units that were part of the same combat. If the unit is not in a legal position, backtrack the move to the unit's last legal position where it follows the Unit Spacing rule.

Figure 34 shows a simple example of a Pursuit Move, figure 35 illustrates a case where two units are Pursuing into an enemy unit, and figure 36 introduces more complex cases.

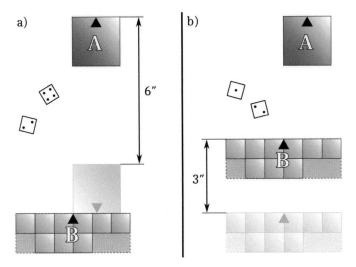

Figure 34: Simple example of a Pursuit.

a) Unit A Breaks from Combat. It Pivots to face away from unit B, and then moves the Flee Distance forwards.

b) Unit B Pursues. It does not need to Pivot as it is already facing the same direction as unit A, and moves the Pursuit Distance forwards.

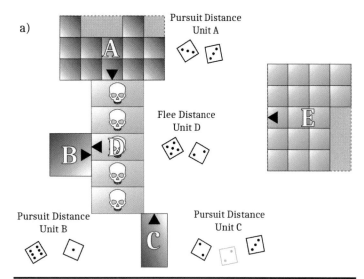

Pursuit Distance Unit A

Flee Distance Unit D

Pursuit Distance Unit B

Pursuit Distance Unit C

Figure 35: Example of two units Pursuing into the same enemy unit.

a) Unit D loses the combat, Breaks, and Flees 7″. The owner of the winning units chooses to roll for unit A's Pursuit Distance first. 6″ is not enough to catch the Fleeing unit. Unit B's Pursuit Distance is 7″, so it is equal or higher than unit D's Flee Distance: the Fleeing unit is immediately destroyed. Unit C's Pursuit Distance is 5″.

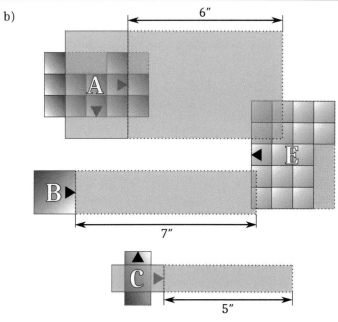

b) When checking which units will Charge an enemy unit during their Pursuit, before moving any Pursuing unit, it turns out that both unit A and unit B will Charge unit E, so both units declare a Charge against unit E. Unit C will not Charge any enemy units.

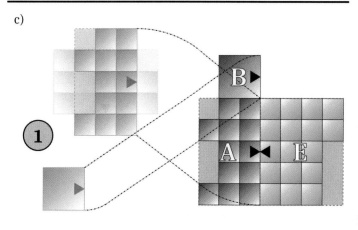

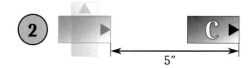

c) Now units A and B perform their Pursuit Moves first. During this move, they can move through one another as they treat each other as Open Terrain. Otherwise they move using the normal rules for Moving Chargers (one Wheel allowed, Maximising Contact). In order to maximise the number of models and units in base contact, unit A aligns its Front Facing with unit E's, while unit B moves into corner to corner contact with unit E. Afterwards unit C Pivots and moves its Pursuit Distance straight forward.

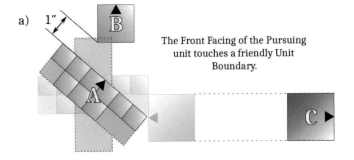

a)

The Front Facing of the Pursuing unit touches a friendly Unit Boundary.

Figure 36: Examples of Pursuits.

a) Unit C is in unit A's Flank. Unit A wins combat, unit C Breaks and Flees, unit A Pursues. Pivoting unit A would make its Front Facing overlap a friendly unit, unit B. The Pivot is instead made as close as possible to the intended direction and the Pursuit Move ends.

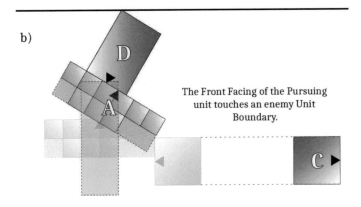

b)

The Front Facing of the Pursuing unit touches an enemy Unit Boundary.

b) Unit C is in unit A's Flank. Unit A wins combat, unit C Breaks and Flees, unit A Pursues. Pivoting unit A would make its Front Facing overlap an enemy unit, unit D. Unit A is removed from the Battlefield and then placed back on the Battlefield with its Front Facing in base contact with the Charged unit D's Front Facing, maximising contact while keeping the Centre of the unit as close as possible to its starting position.

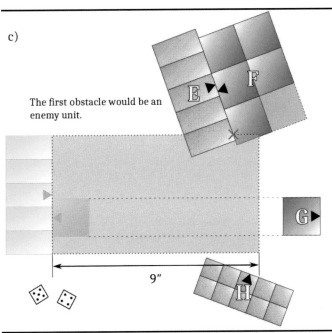

c)

The first obstacle would be an enemy unit.

9"

c) Unit G Breaks and Flees from unit E. No obstacles are encountered during the Pivot. The first obstacle unit E would encounter during its move ahead is unit F. Unit E must now perform a Charge Move against unit F, Maximising Contact as usual.

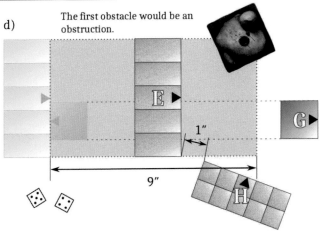

d)

The first obstacle would be an obstruction.

1"

9"

d) Unit G Breaks and Flees from unit E. No obstacles are encountered during the Pivot. The first obstacle unit E would encounter during its move ahead is Impassable Terrain. Unit E is moved into contact with the Impassable Terrain. However, this position breaks the Unit Spacing rule. Unit E's Pursuit move is backtracked to its last legal position.

15.H.d Pursuing off the Board

When a unit Pursues off the Board, it will leave the Battlefield and will return during the owner's next Movement Phase, using the rules for arriving Ambushers (see "Ambush", page 93), with the following exceptions:

- It automatically arrives.
- It must be placed with its rear rank centred on a point at which it contacted the Board Edge, or as close as possible.
- It must arrive in the same formation as it left.
- It does not count as destroyed at the end of the game, nor does it lose Scoring.

15.H.e Post-Combat Pivot and Post-Combat Reform

After Pursuing and Fleeing units have been moved, the other units that were Engaged in the same Combat but are now unengaged may now perform one of the manoeuvres below (in an order determined by the rules for "Simultaneous Effects", page 5).

15.H.e.1 Post-Combat Pivot

The unit Pivots around its Centre and/or may reorganise models with the Front Rank rule (they must still be in legal positions).

15.H.e.2 Post-Combat Reform

The unit performs a Reform manoeuvre. If it does, the unit doesn't count as Scoring for claiming Secondary Objectives until the start of the following Player Turn and may not declare any Charges in the following Player Turn.

15.1 Combat Reforms

Each unit still Engaged in Combat after all Fleeing and Pursuing units have moved, and after Post-Combat Pivots and Post-Combat Reforms have been performed, now performs a Combat Reform.

- Units on the losing side of the combat must pass a Discipline Test in order to do so. Apply the same modifiers as for the previous Break Test (i.e. apply the Combat Score difference, unless the unit is Steadfast or Stubborn).

- Units Engaged in more than one Facing can never perform any Combat Reforms.

- After all Discipline tests have been taken, the Active Player decides which player performs their Combat Reforms first. After this player has completed all Combat Reforms with their units (one at a time, in any order), the opponent Combat Reforms their units.

- Each player may choose not to Combat Reform one or more of their units.

When performing a Combat Reform, remove a unit from the Battlefield and place it back, following these restrictions:

- The unit must be placed in a legal formation (following the Unit Spacing rule, etc.).
  - The unit is allowed to come within 0.5″ of units Engaged in the same Combat, but it cannot move into base contact with enemy units that it was not in base contact with before the Combat Reform.

- The unit must be placed in base contact with all the enemy units it was in base contact before the Combat Reform, and in the same Facing of the enemy unit(s).

- All models in the unit must be placed with their centre within their March Rate from their position before the Combat Reform.

- Characters that were in base contact with an enemy must still be after the Combat Reform.
  - This applies to both enemy and friendly Characters.
  - A Character may end up in base contact with different enemy models than it was before the Combat Reform.

- After each Combat Reform, at least as many models of the Combat Reforming unit must be in base contact with enemy models as there were before.
  - These don't have to be the same models.

Furthermore, after a player has completed all their Combat Reforms, all enemy models that were in base contact with opposing models before the Combat Reform must still be in base contact after the Combat Reform, but they may be Engaged with different models or units.

See figure 37 for an example of Combat Reforms.

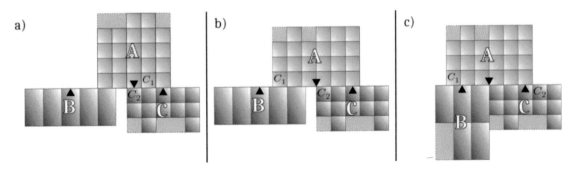

Figure 37: Combat Reforms.

a) At the end of a Round of Combat, the Combined Unit A is Engaged with unit B and the Combined Unit C. All units perform Combat Reforms, starting with unit A.

b) After Unit A's Combat Reform, the unit has added a file to the left, and the Character joined to the unit has moved to the left.

c) During Unit B's Combat Reform, the unit shifts as far as possible to the right and the two models that are not in base contact with enemy models are moved to the second rank. Unit C does not change its position, however the Character joined to the unit moves into a position where it is in base contact only with a single enemy model.

16 Casualties

Models suffering unsaved wounds lose Health Points.

16.A Losing Health Points

16.A.a R&F Models

R&F models except Champions in the same unit share a common Health Pool. If the attack was allocated towards or distributed onto a R&F model, the combined R&F Health Pool loses 1 Health Point for each unsaved wound. If the R&F models have 1 Health Point each, remove one R&F model for each Health Point lost.

If the R&F models have more than 1 Health Point each, remove whole R&F models whenever possible. Keep track of Health Points lost from the Health Pool that are not enough to remove an entire model. These lost Health Points are taken into account for future attacks. For example, a unit of 10 Trolls (3 Health Points each) loses 7 Health Points. Remove two whole models (6 Health Points), leaving 1 lost Health Point which is kept track of. Later, this unit loses 2 Health Points, which is enough to remove a single Troll since 1 Health Point was lost from the previous attack.

If all non-Champion R&F models in a unit are wiped out, any excess lost Health Points are allotted to the Champion (even if it is fighting a Duel). If there is no Champion, the excess Health Point losses are ignored.

If a unit consists of R&F models with different Types and/or Heights, all R&F models with the same Type and Height have their own separate Health Pool.

16.A.b Champions

Even though Champions are R&F models, each Champion has its own Health Pool, and follows the rules for Characters below. If enough Health Points are lost by R&F models in order to wipe out the entire unit, any remaining lost Health Points are allotted to the Champion (even if it is fighting a Duel).

16.A.c Characters

If the attack was allocated towards or distributed onto a Character, the attacked model loses 1 Health Point for each unsaved wound. If the model reaches 0 Health Points, it is removed as a casualty. Keep track of models that have lost Health Points, but not enough to reach 0 Health Points (placing "Health Point markers" next to such models works fine). These lost Health Points will be taken into account for future attacks. If the model is removed as a casualty, any excess Health Point losses are ignored.

16.A.d Excess Health Point Losses

Whenever more Health Point losses are inflicted than there are Health Points in a Health Pool, these excess Health Point losses are ignored.

When caused by simultaneous attacks from models from two or more Health Pools and/or units, it may be necessary to determine which models caused the excess Health Point losses. In this case, the owner of the models that inflicted the Health Point losses gets to decide.

16.A.e Losing the Last Health Point

Certain effects are triggered by models being removed as a casualty, while others are set off by models losing their last Health Point or reaching 0 Health Points. Note that losing the last Health Point does not apply to situations in which a model is directly removed as a casualty, without actually losing any Health Points, like Fleeing off the board or being destroyed after Breaking from Combat.

16.B   Removing Casualties

Whenever the rules tell you to remove models as casualties, remove the models from the Battlefield following the rules below. Models that have been removed as casualties no longer affect the game in any way, but they may award Victory Points to the opponent (see "Victory Conditions", page 85).

16.B.a   Removing R&F Models

If the unit is in multiple ranks, R&F casualties are removed from the rear rank by the owner, in any order they choose.

If the unit is in a single rank, remove models as equally as possible from both sides of the unit. Note that this only applies to each batch of simultaneous attacks.

If a Champion or Character is in a position that would normally be removed as a casualty, remove the next eligible R&F model and slide the Champion and/or Character model(s) into the now empty spot.

16.B.b   Removing R&F Models from Units Engaged in Combat

The removal of casualties from Engaged units follows the general rules for Removing R&F models above. In addition, if the unit is in a single rank, remove casualties from either side of the unit, so that the following conditions are satisfied as best as possible for each batch of simultaneous casualties, in decreasing priority order:

- 1st priority: As few units as possible Drop out of Combat (see "Losing Base Contact", page 69)
- 2nd priority: As few units as possible lose base contact without Dropping out of Combat
- 3rd priority: The number of models in base contact is maximised after nudging all units
- 4th priority: Casualties are removed as equally as possible from both sides of the unit

If it is unavoidable to break one or more of the above conditions, you must avoid breaking the higher priority order conditions, even if this means the total number of conditions you break is higher. As long as all above conditions are satisfied as best as possible, the owner is free to remove casualties as they please. See figure 38 for examples.

16.B.c   Removing Champions and Characters

When Champions and Characters are removed as casualties they are removed from their positions within the unit. Other models are then moved to fill empty spots, following the same guidelines as for casualty removal above. When removing casualties from unengaged units with a single rank, Champions and Characters follow the rules for Matching Bases (see "Front Rank", page 95).

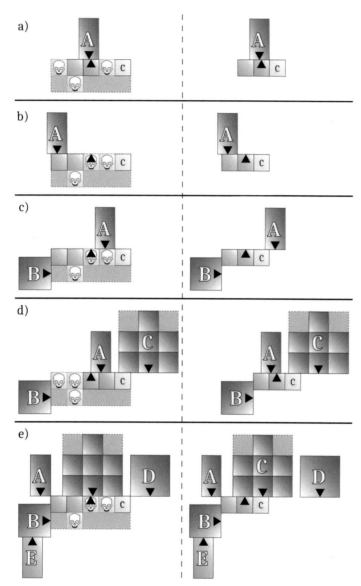

Figure 38: Removing R&F models from units Engaged in Combat.

This figure shows how models are removed as casualties from a unit that is Engaged with one or more enemy units according to Removing R&F Models from Units Engaged in Combat. In all examples, 3 models are removed as casualties from the green Combined Unit containing a Character in its first rank.

a) One of these casualties is the model in the second rank, and the other two have to be removed from both sides of the first rank according to the 4th priority. Since there is a Character on the right side of the unit, the R&F model to its left is removed instead, and the Character is slid into the removed model's spot.

b) In order to maximise the number of models in base contact (3rd priority), the model in the second rank and the two rightmost R&F models from the first rank are removed as casualties. The Character is slid into the spot of a removed R&F model.

c) In order not to have unit B lose base contact by removing casualties (2nd priority), the model in the second rank and the two rightmost R&F models from the first rank are removed as casualties. The Character is slid into the spot of a removed R&F model.

d) In order not to cause any units to Drop out of Combat (1st priority), the model in the second rank and the two leftmost R&F models from the first rank are removed as casualties. Unit B loses contact but is nudged back into combat (see "Losing Base Contact", page 69).

e) In order to cause as few units as possible to Drop out of Combat (1st priority), the model in the second rank and the two rightmost R&F models from the first rank are removed as casualties. The Character is slid into the spot of a removed R&F model. Unit D loses contact and cannot be nudged back into combat, so that it Drops out of Combat (see "Losing Base Contact", page 69).

17 Psychology

17.A Panic Test

A Panic Test is a Discipline Test that a unit has to take immediately after any of the following situations arise:

- A friendly unit is destroyed within 6″ of the unit (including Fleeing off the board).
- A friendly unit Breaks from Combat within 6″ of the unit.
- A friendly unit Flees through the unit's Unit Boundary.
- In a single phase, the unit suffers Health Point losses equal to or greater than 25% of the number of Health Points that it had at the start of the phase. This does not apply to single model units that started the game as a single model (i.e. with a starting number of 1 model on the Army List).

Unless specifically stated otherwise, units that fail a Panic Test immediately Flee directly away from the closest enemy unit (Centre of Unit to Centre of Unit). If several enemy units are equally close, randomise which one the unit will Flee away from. If there are no enemy units on the Battlefield, randomise the direction. If the Panic Test was caused by any of the cases listed below, the unit Flees directly away from the enemy unit that caused the Panic Test (Centre of Unit to Centre of Unit).

- A spell cast by an enemy model
- A Model Rule on an enemy model (such as Terror)
- Losing 25% or more Health Points, and the final wounds causing the Health Point losses to reach or go above 25% were due to an attack by an enemy unit

If several units have to take a Panic Test at the same time, take all Panic Tests before performing any Flee Moves caused by failed Panic Tests.

Units do not take Panic Tests if they are Engaged in Combat, if they are already Fleeing, or if they already passed a Panic Test during this phase.

17.B Shaken

Under certain circumstances, models may become Shaken. The most common situations are:

- Charging a Fleeing unit (page 43)
- Failing a Charge (page 46)
- Rallying a Fleeing Unit (page 50)
- Failing a Fear Test (see "Fear", page 94)
- War Machines failing a Panic Test (see "War Machine", page 101)
- War Machines suffering a Jammed Misfire Effect (page 109)

A Shaken model cannot perform any of the following actions:

- Declare Charges
- Pursuit
- Overrun
- Advance Move
- March Move
- Reform (it can Combat Reform and Post-Combat Reform)
- Random Movement

- Shooting Attack

17.C Fleeing

A unit is considered Fleeing from the moment:

- It fails a Break Test (after potential rerolls)
- It fails a Panic Test (after potential rerolls)
- Its Flee Distance is rolled

As soon as a unit passes its Rally Test, it is no longer considered Fleeing.

When a unit is Fleeing, it cannot perform any voluntary actions (a voluntary action is an action that a unit would have the option to not perform). This includes (but is not limited to):

- Declare Charges
- Charge Reactions other than Flee
- Move in any way other than a Flee Move
- Shoot
- Channel
- Cast spells or activate One use only Special Items which need to be activated voluntarily

Models cannot receive Commanding Presence or Rally Around the Flag from a Fleeing model.

17.D Decimated

A unit is considered Decimated if the sum of the Health Points of its models, including Characters that are part of the unit, is 25% or less of its starting Health Points (the number taken from the Army List, regardless of any Characters in the unit). Decimated units must take their Rally Test at half their Discipline, rounding fractions up (this is not considered a Characteristic modifier).

For example, if a unit with Discipline 8 started the game with 40 models with 1 Health Point each, is reduced to 9 models and Flees, it takes Rally Tests at Discipline 4. However, if a Character with Discipline 8 and 2 Health Points is part of the unit, the Combined Unit would instead take its Rally Test at Discipline 8.

18   Victory Conditions

At the end of the game, players determine the winner of the battle. For this purpose, calculate each player's Victory Points, check if any player scored the Secondary Objective, and distribute the Battle Points accordingly as described below. Of course players may agree to use a different method to determine the winner, e.g. by creating custom scenarios that set specific goals for each player to claim victory.

18.A   Scoring Victory Points

At the end of each game, each player is awarded a number of Victory Points (VP) according to the rules below.

Destroyed Units	For each enemy unit that has been removed as a casualty, you gain a number of **VP equal to its Point Cost.**
Fleeing Units	For each enemy unit that is Fleeing at the end of the game, you gain a number of **VP equal to half its Point Cost, rounding fractions up.**
Shattered Units	For each enemy unit that is at 25% or less of its starting Health Points (of the number taken from the Army List) at the end of the game, you gain a number of **VP equal to half its Point Cost, rounding fractions up**. Characters are counted separately from the units they have joined. Note that if an enemy unit is both Fleeing and Shattered, you gain a number of VP equal to the unit's total Point Cost.
Defeated General	If the enemy General was removed as a casualty, you gain **200 VP**.
Defeated Battle Standard Bearer	If the enemy Battle Standard Bearer was removed as a casualty, you gain **200 VP**.

18.B   Scoring Secondary Objectives

The Secondary Objective selected at the start of the game can grant extra Battle Points (see "Secondary Objectives", page 35, and table 8 below).

18.C   Who is the Winner?

Once all Victory Points are added together, a total of 20 Battle Points are divided between the players, depending on the Victory Point Difference. Calculate the Victory Point Difference and use table 8 below to convert the Victory Points into Battle Points. The winner of the Secondary Objective gains 3 additional Battle Points while the loser of the Secondary Objective loses 3 Battle Points. In case there is no winner, the Secondary Objective ends in a draw and no additional Battle Points are awarded to either player.

18.C.a   Optional Simplified Rules for Determining the Winner

Winning the Secondary Objective awards the winner a number of Victory Points equal to 20% of the Army Points. Once all Victory Points are added together, compare the two results.

- If the Victory Point Difference is less than 10% of the Army Points, the result is a **Draw**.
- If the Victory Point Difference is at least 10% and up to 50% of the Army Points, the result is a **Win** for the player who scored higher.
- If the Victory Point Difference is more than 50% of the Army Points, the result is a **Massacre** for the player who scored higher.

Victory Point Difference		Battle Points	
Percentage of Army Points	(if playing with 4500 Army Points)	**Winner**	**Loser**
0–5%	0–225	10	10
>5–10%	226–450	11	9
>10–20%	451–900	12	8
>20–30%	901–1350	13	7
>30–40%	1351–1800	14	6
>40–50%	1801–2250	15	5
>50–70%	2251–3150	16	4
>70%	>3150	17	3
Winning Secondary Objective		+3	−3

Table 8: Victory Point Difference and Battle Points.

19   Model Classification

19.A   Classification of Models

All models have a Height and a Type, defined in their unit entry.

19.A.a   Height

Models come in three Heights, which are connected to the following rules:

	Standard	Large	Gigantic
Model Rules	None	Stomp Attacks (1)	Fear Massive Bulk Stomp Attacks (D6) Terror Towering Presence
Full Ranks Minimum number of models required to form Full Ranks	5	3	1
Supporting Attacks Maximum number of Supporting Attacks	1	3	5
Dangerous Terrain Number of D6 rolled when performing Dangerous Terrain Tests	1	2	3

19.A.b   Type

Models come in four Types, which are associated with the following rules:

Infantry	Beast	Cavalry	Construct
None	Swiftstride	Cannot be Stomped Swiftstride Tall	Cannot use Stomp Attacks Chariot

19.A.c   Models on Foot and Mounted Models

Certain spells and rules affect models on foot and mounted models differently.

Models that don't include any model parts with Harnessed are considered to be on foot.

Models with at least one model part with Harnessed are considered to be mounted.

19.B Character Mounts

Many Characters can select mounts from the mount section of their Army Book. When a Character, referred to as the rider, selects a mount, apply the following rules:

19.B.1 Height, Type, and Base

Always use the Height, Type, and base of the mount.

19.B.2 Offensive Characteristics

Rider and mount use their own respective Offensive Characteristics.

19.B.3 Global and Defensive Characteristics

The Multipart Model has a single set of Global Characteristics and a single set of Defensive Characteristics. Always use the values in the mount's profile, except when that value is "C". In this case, "C" refers to the value in the Character's profile which is used instead. Sometimes, a value is written as "C + X". In this case, use the Character's value, increased by X.

For example, if a Character (Armour 0) rides a horse (Armour C + 2), wears Heavy Armour (+2 Armour), and carries a Shield (+1 Armour), the Multipart Model has an Armour equal to: 0 + 2 + 2 + 1 = 5.

19.B.4 Model Rules

Model Rules connected to specific model parts (such as Attack Attributes, Special Attacks, and weapons) are only applied to this model part. Other Model Rules (such as Universal Rules, Character, Armour, and Personal Protections) are applied to the Multipart Model as normal.

Remember that models with Massive Bulk (all models of Gigantic Height) ignore Armour and Personal Protections from the rider.

19.C Classification of Units

Some rules call for a unit's Height or Type, e.g. for determining how many models are required for Full Ranks. In case a unit contains a mix of different Heights the unit's Height is the same as that of the largest fraction of its models. Likewise, a unit's Type is the same as that of the largest fraction of its models. In case of a tie, the opponent chooses which fraction to use.

20   Terrain

20.A   Terrain Types

20.A.a   Dangerous Terrain (X)

A model must take a Dangerous Terrain Test if it is in contact with a Terrain Feature that counts as Dangerous Terrain at any point during its March, Charge, Failed Charge, Flee, Pursuit, or Overrun Move. Take a Dangerous Terrain Test by rolling a number of D6 depending on the model's Height and Model Rules:

	Standard	Large	Gigantic	Chariot
Number of D6 rolled	1	2	3	+1

For each dice that rolled equal to or below X (where X is the value stated in brackets), the model suffers a hit with Armour Penetration 10 that wounds automatically.

Note that:

- Dangerous Terrain Tests are taken as soon as the model is in contact with the relevant Terrain. If it does not matter exactly when a model is removed as a casualty, take all Dangerous Terrain Tests for a unit at the same time.

- Hits suffered from Dangerous Terrain Tests are distributed onto the model's Health Pool.

- A model never takes more than one Dangerous Terrain Test for the same Terrain Feature during a single move, but it might have to take several Dangerous Terrain Tests caused by different Terrain Features or abilities.

20.A.b   Opaque Terrain

Line of Sight cannot be drawn through Opaque Terrain, but can be drawn into it. Models always ignore any Terrain they are inside for drawing Line of Sight.

20.A.c   Covering Terrain

Like models, Terrain Features may contribute to Cover when obscuring a fraction of the Target Facing or the Target Point from the enemy's Line of Sight (see "Cover", page 62, and remember that Cover modifiers only apply if more than half of the Target Facing or the Target Point is obscured by Cover).

For the purpose of counting as Cover, Terrain Features may distinguish:

- Targets obscured **behind** the Terrain Feature. These units must have more than half of their Target Facing or their Target Point off the Terrain Feature, and the part of the Terrain Feature obscuring Line of Sight must be between the shooting model and its target.

- Targets obscured **inside** the Terrain Feature. These units must have more than half of their Target Facing or their Target Point inside the Terrain Feature.

- Targets obscured **behind and/or inside** the Terrain Feature: there is no need to determine where more than half of these units' Target Facing or their Target Point lies (as long as it is obscured).

Models always ignore any Terrain they are inside for drawing Line of Sight.

20.B   Terrain Features

A Terrain Feature is a topographical area on the Battlefield that may be a mixture of Dangerous, Impassable, Opaque, or Covering Terrain and may possess its own set of rules.

20.B.a   Open Terrain

Open Terrain normally doesn't have any effect on Line of Sight, Cover modifiers, or movement. All parts of the board that are not covered by any other kind of Terrain are considered to be Open Terrain.

20.B.b   Fields

Fields can be represented in the game for example by meadows or agricultural fields.

Types	Fields are Covering Terrain for units **inside** them.
Cover	Fields contribute to Soft Cover, except for models with Towering Presence.

20.B.c   Forests

Forests can be represented in the game for example by jungles, brushwoods, or coniferous forests.

Types	Forests are Covering Terrain for units **inside and/or behind them**, and Dangerous Terrain (1) for Cavalry, Constructs, and units making a Flying Movement.
Cover	Forests contribute to Soft Cover.
Broken Ranks	Units with more than half of their models with the centre of their base inside a Forest can never be Steadfast, unless specifically stated otherwise.
Guerilla Warfare	Units consisting entirely of Infantry models with Light Troops are **Stubborn** if more than half of their models are inside a Forest with the centre of their bases, unless any model in the unit has Towering Presence and/or Fly.

20.B.d   Hills

Hills can be represented in the game for example by elevated plateaus or burial mounds.

Types	Hills are Opaque Terrain. Hills are Covering Terrain for units **behind** them.
Cover	Hills contribute to Soft Cover for targets behind **but partially on** them. Hills contribute to Hard Cover for targets behind **and entirely off** them.
Elevated Position	Models with the centre of their base on a Hill are considered to be Elevated. Ignore all intervening non-Elevated models if you are: • drawing Line of Sight to or from Elevated models. • determining Cover when shooting with: – Elevated models. – non-Elevated models at units which have more than half of their models Elevated.
Charging Downhill	A unit initiating a Charge Move with more than half of its models with the centre of their base on a Hill towards an enemy with more than half of its models with the centre of their base off a Hill must reroll failed Charge Range rolls.

20.B.e Impassable Terrain

Impassable Terrain can be represented in the game for example by monoliths, massive boulders, or buildings.

Types	Impassable Terrain is Opaque Terrain.
Cover	Impassable Terrain contributes to Hard Cover for units behind it.
Mission Impassible	Models cannot move into or through Impassable Terrain.

20.B.f Ruins

Ruins can be represented in the game for example by rubble or abandoned farmsteads.

Types	Ruins are Covering Terrain for units **inside** them, Dangerous Terrain (2) for Cavalry and Constructs, and Dangerous Terrain (1) for any other unit. Units with Skirmisher automatically pass Dangerous Terrain Tests caused by Ruins.
Cover	Ruins contribute to Hard Cover, except for models with Towering Presence.

20.B.g Walls

Walls can be represented in the game for example by wooden barricades, stone walls, or hedges.

Types	Walls are Covering Terrain for models **behind** them while Defending the Wall (see below) and Dangerous Terrain (2) for Constructs.
Cover	Walls contribute to Hard Cover, except for models with Towering Presence.
Defending a Wall	In order to Defend a Wall, more than half of a unit's Front Facing must be in contact with it.
Fortified Position	Units Defending a Wall gain **Distracting** against Close Combat Attacks from Charging enemies in their Front Facing.

20.B.h Water Terrain

Water Terrain can be represented in the game for example by ponds, swamps, or rivers.

Types	Water Terrain is Dangerous Terrain (1) for Standard Height models on foot.
Broken Ranks	Units with more than half of their models with the centre of their base inside Water Terrain can never be Steadfast, unless specifically stated otherwise.
Doused Flames	All Melee Attacks against or by models in units with more than half of their models with the centre of their base inside Water Terrain are no longer Flaming Attacks (if they were before).

20.C Board Edge

The Board Edge represents the boundaries of the game. A unit is allowed to temporarily and partially move off the board (during any move) with by the following restrictions:

- The unit's Front Facing must remain entirely on the board at all times, except during align moves.

- The unit must finish its move with its Unit Boundary entirely on the board.

21 Model Rules

Model Rules are rules that are applied to individual models or model parts, as described in their unit entry. They are divided into the following categories: Universal Rules, Character, Personal Protections, Armour Equipment, Weapons, Attack Attributes, and Special Attacks.

Duplicated Model Rules

Sometimes a model or model part may have the same Model Rule more than once, for example when a model gains a Model Rule during the game that it already had before. In this case, the effects of the duplicated Model Rule do not stack and do not offer any additional benefit, unless specifically stated otherwise.

If the duplicated Model Rule has different values in brackets (X), use the highest value.

If X is the result of a dice roll, you may instead choose which version to use (before rolling any dice).

If X is not a value, the Model Rules are not considered to be duplicates of the same Model Rule and both rules are applied (e.g. Hatred (against Infantry) and Hatred (against Cavalry) are considered two different Model Rules, so both effects are applied).

21.A   Universal Rules

If at least one model part has a Universal Rule, the entire Multipart Model is affected by it.

For example, in case of a Character with the Strider Universal Rule on a Character mount without this Universal Rule, all model parts of the Multipart Model (Character and mount) benefit from Strider.

21.A.a   List of Universal Rules

21.A.a.1 Ambush

Units with Ambush may be deployed using Special Deployment rules. All units that will be deployed using the Ambush rule must be declared at step 8 of the Pre-Game Sequence (after Spell Selection), starting with the player that chose their Deployment Zone. Deploy your army as usual, but without the Ambushing units. Starting with your Player Turn 2, immediately after step 2 of the Movement Phase Sequence (after moving units with Random Movement), roll a dice for each of your Ambushing units. After rolling for all Ambushing units, all units that rolled 3+ enter the Battlefield from any Board Edge. Place the arriving units with their Rear Facing in contact and aligned with the Board Edge. Ambushers are subject to the following rules and restrictions:

- Ambushing models can neither March Move during the Movement Phase in which they arrive, nor can they voluntarily end that Movement Phase farther away from the Board Edge that they arrived from than their March Rate.

- Ambushing models count as having moved during the turn they arrive on the Battlefield.

- If an Ambushing unit has not entered the Battlefield before the end of the game (e.g. due to failing all its 3+ rolls), the unit counts as destroyed.

- An Ambushing unit that enters the Battlefield on Game Turn 4 or later loses Scoring.

- An Ambushing Character may Ambush within an Ambushing unit that it is allowed to join (declare this when declaring which units are Ambushing). Roll only one dice for the Combined Unit.

- Until arriving on the Battlefield, Ambushing units cannot perform any actions at all, and all their Special Items, rules, and abilities don't work while off the board.

21.A.a.2 Battle Standard Bearer – One of a Kind

An army may only include a single Battle Standard Bearer. The model gains **Rally Around the Flag** and **Not a Leader**. If the model has the option to buy Special Items, it is allowed to buy up to two Banner Enchantments.

21.A.a.3 Bodyguard (X)

While a Character is joined to a unit in which at least one model has Bodyguard, that Character gains **Stubborn**. When Characters or Character types are stated in brackets, Bodyguard only works for the specified Characters or Character types.

21.A.a.4 Channel (X)

During step 3 of the Magic Phase Sequence, each of the Active Player's models with Channel may add X Veil Tokens to its owner's Veil Token pool. This Universal Rule is cumulative, adding the X of each instance of Channel to the model's total Channel value (e.g. a model with Channel (1) and Channel (2) is treated like a model with Channel (3)).

21.A.a.5 Chariot

The model must roll an additional D6 when taking Dangerous Terrain Tests. A model with Chariot can only be part of a unit consisting entirely of models with Chariot, unless specifically stated otherwise.

21.A.a.6 Commanding Presence

All Generals have the Commanding Presence Universal Rule. The Discipline of all units within 12″ of a friendly non-Fleeing model with Commanding Presence may be **set** to the Discipline value of that model (this ability follows the normal rules for "Values Set to a Fixed Number", page 16, meaning that effects modifying the Discipline of the model with Commanding Presence are applied before setting the recipient model's Discipline to that value; this value may then be further modified).

21.A.a.7   Engineer (X+)

Once per Shooting Phase, an unengaged Engineer may select a single War Machine within 6″ that has not fired yet to gain the following effects:

- **Set** the Aim of one of the War Machine's Artillery Weapons to the value given in brackets (X+).

- You may reroll the roll on the Misfire Table.

- You may reroll the dice (all of them or none) for determining the number of hits of a Flamethrower Artillery Weapon.

21.A.a.8 Fear

Units in base contact with one or more enemy models with Fear suffer −1 Discipline. At the start of each Round of Combat, such units must take a Discipline Test, called a Fear Test. If this test is failed, the models in the unit are Shaken and Close Combat Attacks made by models in the unit suffer −1 to hit, while Close Combat Attacks allocated towards models in the unit gain +1 to hit. These effects apply until the end of the Round of Combat. Models that have Fear themselves are immune to the effects of Fear.

21.A.a.9 Fearless

If more than half of a unit's models are Fearless, the unit automatically passes Panic Tests and cannot declare a Flee Charge Reaction, unless already Fleeing. Models that are Fearless are also immune to the effects of Fear.

21.A.a.10 Feigned Flight

Units consisting entirely of models with Feigned Flight do not become Shaken if they voluntarily choose Flee as Charge Reaction and pass their Rally Test in their next Player Turn. The Reform after Rallying in this case does not prevent the unit from moving nor from shooting, but the unit still counts as having moved. This rule does not apply if a unit fails to rally on the next friendly Player Turn or Flees involuntarily (e.g. as the result of a failed Panic Test, or if it was already Fleeing when being Charged).

21.A.a.11   Fly (X, Y)

Units composed entirely of models with Fly may use Flying Movement during Charge Moves, Failed Charge Moves, Advance Moves, and March Moves. When a unit uses Flying Movement, substitute its models' Advance Rate with the first value given in brackets (X), and their March Rate with the second value given in brackets (Y). A unit using Flying Movement ignores all Terrain Features and units during the Flying Movement. Note that:

- It must follow the Unit Spacing rule at the end of the move.

- It is affected by the Terrain Features from which it takes off and in which it lands.

- All modifiers to ground movement values also apply to a model's Fly values, unless specifically stated otherwise.

- When declaring a Charge with a unit with Fly, you must declare if the unit will not use Flying Movement for the Charge Move.

- A Failed Charge Move of a unit with Fly must use the type of movement (ground or Flying) that was chosen when the Charge was declared. If the unit would end its Failed Charge Move inside another unit's Unit Boundary or inside Impassable Terrain, backtrack the move to the unit's last legal position where it follows the Unit Spacing rule.

21.A.a.12 Frenzy

At the start of the Charge Phase, each of your units with at least one model with Frenzy that could declare a Charge against an enemy unit within the unit's Advance Rate +7″ must take a Discipline Test, called a Frenzy Test. If the test is failed, the whole unit must declare a Charge this Player Turn if possible.

Frenzy Tests and Restrain Pursuit Tests taken by units with at least one model with Frenzy are subject to Maximised Roll.

If there are different Advance Rates available in the unit, the Advance Rate used for the Frenzy Test and for the Charge Range is determined as follows:

- If a model has more than one Advance Rate (e.g. due to Fly), the model must use the Advance Rate that has the highest chance of completing the Charge.
- If a unit contains models with different Advance Rates, the unit must use the highest Advance Rate that all models in the unit can use (which will usually be the lowest Advance Rate in the unit).

For example, a model with Advance Rate 2″ and Fly (8″, 16″) must use the Advance Rate from Fly. And if a Character in a Combined Unit has Advance Rate 4″ while the R&F models have 6″, the Combined Unit must use Advance Rate 4″. Note that when a unit is forced to declare a Charge due to a failed Frenzy Test, it is not forced to Charge the enemy unit that triggered the Frenzy Test.

21.A.a.13 Front Rank

Front Rank specifies where in a unit the model may be placed and how the model moves inside its unit.

A model with Front Rank must always be placed as far forwards as possible in its unit. This normally means that it must be placed in the first rank unless specifically stated otherwise.

When making an Advance Move, March Move, or Reform with a unit that includes models with Front Rank, these models can be reorganised into a new position (still as far forwards as possible) as part of the move. This counts towards the distance moved by the unit (measure the distance from the starting position to the ending position of the centre of the model with Front Rank to determine how far it has moved).

A model with Front Rank can either have a Matching Base or a Mismatching Base.

Matching Bases

In Combined Units containing Characters and R&F models, a Character is considered to have a Matching Base if:

- The model has the same base size as the R&F models.
- The model's base is the same size as a multiple of the R&F models' bases (such as a 40×40 mm base in a 20×20 mm unit).

For Combined Units consisting entirely of Characters, Matching Bases are determined differently as these units do not contain any R&F models. The R&F base size for the purposes of Matching Bases must:

- Correspond to the base size of at least one of the Characters
- Result in as few Characters as possible having Mismatching Bases; the owner chooses in case of a tie

For example, in a unit consisting of a 25×25 mm Character and two 25×50 mm Characters, that base size is 25×25 mm, as it does not result in any Mismatching Bases in the unit.

If the first rank is occupied by models with Front Rank, a model with Matching Base is placed in the second rank instead. If this rank is also occupied by models with Front Rank, it is placed in the third rank, and so on. Matching Bases are subject to the following rules and restrictions:

- If the model has a larger base than the R&F models, it is considered to be in all ranks its base occupies for the purposes of calculating Full Ranks. For calculating the number of models in the unit's ranks (e.g. for Full Ranks, Line Formation, Area Attack), the large base counts as the number of models it replaces.
- If a model with a Matching Base has a longer base than the R&F models in the unit, the unit is allowed to have more than one incomplete rank if all incomplete ranks after the first consist entirely of models with such bases (for instance the rear parts of long bases such as War Platforms are allowed to form several incomplete ranks).
- A model cannot join a unit that has more than one rank if its base is wider than the unit it wishes to join, nor can a unit Reform into a formation that is narrower than any model joined to the unit.

If a model with Front Rank moves inside or leaves a unit that has more than one rank, or if it is removed from such a unit as a casualty, the gap the model leaves must be filled with models without Front Rank. If there aren't any models without Front Rank available, move models with Front Rank instead. After filling a gap, sometimes models with Front Rank must be redistributed in order for all such models to be as far forwards as possible. When this happens, move as few models as possible in order to have all models with Front Rank as far forwards as possible.

If a model with Front Rank moves inside or leaves a unit that has a single rank, or if it is removed from such a unit as a casualty, gaps may be created in the unit. If this leads to an illegal formation (there can only be gaps in an incomplete rear rank; see "Units", page 8), slide as few models as possible to fill the now empty spot. In case of a draw, i.e. if the model was positioned in the middle of the rank, the owner decides which half of the remaining models to slide.

Mismatching Bases

Anything that is not a Matching Base is a Mismatching Base (such as a 50×75 mm base inside a 25×50 mm unit).

A model with Mismatching Base is always placed in base contact to the side of the unit, aligned with its front. Only two Mismatching Bases can be joined to a single unit (one at each side). These models are considered to be only in the first rank, but are ignored when counting the number of models in each rank in order to establish the number of Full Ranks and whether or not a unit is in Line Formation. They form a file of one model each.

During Advance Moves, March Moves, or Reforms, models with Mismatching Bases can only be moved to the other side of the unit as part of the move.

Figure 39 shows how models with Front Rank can be placed in a complex case.

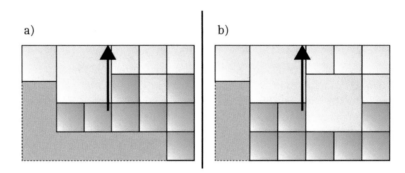

Figure 39: Illustration of the Front Rank rule.

Yellow models have Front Rank, green models do not.

a) A Character on a Mismatching Base is placed next to the unit. Characters on Matching Bases are placed inside the unit, as far forwards as possible. This unit is considered to have 3 Full Ranks.

b) When a model with Front Rank joins the unit, the small model with Front Rank in the second rank must be moved to the side in order to have all models with Front Rank as far forwards as possible.

21.A.a.14 Ghost Step

The model may choose to treat all Terrain Features as Open Terrain for movement purposes, but must follow the Unit Spacing rule upon the completion of its moves. It can never end its move inside Impassable Terrain. If this would be the case, backtrack the move to the unit's last legal position (unless Fleeing, in which case the normal rules for "Flee Moves", page 50 apply).

In addition, the model automatically passes Dangerous Terrain Tests taken due to Terrain.

21.A.a.15 Insignificant

Units consisting entirely of Insignificant models only cause Panic Tests on friendly units in which half the models or more are Insignificant. Units with Insignificant R&F models can only be joined by Insignificant Characters.

21.A.a.16 Light Troops

A unit composed entirely of models with Light Troops applies the following rules for Advance Moves and March Moves:

- The unit may perform any number of Reforms, at any time during the move, and in any order. This does not prevent models with Light Troops from shooting this Player Turn.
- The unit can move backwards and sideways as if moving forwards (i.e. up to its Advance/March Rate), but cannot leave the board with any part of its Unit Boundary.
- The unit cannot perform any Wheels.

In addition:

- Units composed entirely of models with Light Troops gain **March and Shoot**.
- Units with more than half of their models with Light Troops always count as having 0 Full Ranks.
- Infantry Characters gain Light Troops while joined to Infantry units of the same Height with Light Troops.

21.A.a.17 Magic Resistance (X)

Learned Spells and Bound Spells targeting at least one enemy unit with one or more models with Magic Resistance suffer a –X modifier to their casting roll (where X is given in brackets). This is an exception to the Casting and Dispelling Modifier rule. If there are different X values that could be used, use the highest value.

21.A.a.18 Massive Bulk

If the model is mounted by a Character, ignore the rider's Armour Equipment (including Armour Enchantments) and Personal Protections, unless specifically stated otherwise (such as Armour Enchantments that affect the bearer's model).

21.A.a.19 Not a Leader

The model cannot be the General.

21.A.a.20 Protean Magic

During Spell Selection, the Wizard must select its spells from the Learned Spell 1 of each Path it has access to, as well as the Hereditary Spell of its army. This rule overrides the Spell Selection rules for Wizard Apprentices, Adepts, and Masters.

21.A.a.21 Rally Around the Flag

All units within 12″ of a friendly non-Fleeing model with Rally Around the Flag may reroll failed Discipline Tests.

21.A.a.22 Random Movement (X)

At the end of step 2 of the Movement Phase Sequence (after Rallying Fleeing Units), a non-Fleeing unit with Random Movement must move using the rules for Pursuing units, with the following exceptions, which only apply in the Movement Phase, unless specifically stated otherwise:

- It **always** moves the distance stated in brackets (X), which is also used for Flee Distance and Pursuit Distance (including Overruns).
- It can choose which direction to Pivot in before rolling the Pursuit Distance.
- It cannot move off the Board Edge.
- It does not take Dangerous Terrain Tests unless Charging.

There are several restrictions connected with Random Movement:

- The unit cannot move normally in the Movement Phase (Advance, March, Reform) and cannot declare Charges in the Charge Phase. Whenever it requires a March Rate (e.g. when Post-Combat Reforming), use the potential maximum value of X as its March Rate.
- The unit cannot perform Magical Moves.

- The unit loses Swiftstride and can never gain it (but X can be affected by Maximised/Minimised Roll from other sources).

- Characters with Random Movement cannot join units, and units with Random Movement cannot be joined by Characters. Note that Characters that are part of a Combined Unit when the unit gains Random Movement will gain Random Movement too as they are already part of that unit.

- If the unit has several instances of Random Movement, use the one with the lowest average (the owner chooses in case of a tie).

21.A.a.23 Scoring

Units with at least one model with Scoring are considered to be Scoring Units, which are used for winning Secondary Objectives (see "Secondary Objectives", page 35). Every army needs Scoring Units to be able to complete Secondary Objectives, which is why units with Scoring are marked in the Army Books with a special pennant icon:

Scoring can be lost during the game:

- A unit that is Fleeing loses Scoring for as long as it is Fleeing.

- An Ambushing unit that enters the Battlefield on Game Turn 4 or later loses Scoring for the rest of the game.

- A unit that has performed a Post-Combat Reform loses Scoring until the start of the following Player Turn.

- A Vanguarding model loses Scoring until the end of Game Turn 1.

21.A.a.24 Scout

Units with Scout may be deployed using Special Deployment rules. All units that will be deployed using the Scout rule must be declared at step 8 of the Pre-Game Sequence (after Spell Selection), starting with the player that chose their Deployment Zone. Scout deployment is conducted on Step 5 of the Deployment Phase (Deploy Scouting Units). If both players have Scouting units, alternate unit placement (one unit at a time), starting with the player who first completed their normal deployment. Scouting units have three deployment options:

- Fully inside your Deployment Zone, using the normal deployment rules

- Anywhere on the Battlefield at least 18" away from enemy units

- Anywhere on the Battlefield fully inside a Field, Forest, Ruins, or Water Terrain Feature and at least 12" away from enemy units

Scouting units that aren't placed fully inside their Deployment Zone may not declare Charges in the first Player Turn of the first Game Turn (there are no Scout Charge restrictions after the first Player Turn).

21.A.a.25 Skirmisher

The model can always use Shooting Attacks from any rank (models with Skirmisher are not limited to shooting from first and second rank).

Units with at least one R&F model with Skirmisher are formed into a skirmish formation. They are not placed in base contact with each other. Instead, models are placed with a 12.5 mm distance (roughly half an inch) between them. This gap is considered part of the unit for Cover purposes, and will have the same Height as the models in the unit. Other than this gap between models, units with Skirmisher follow the normal rules for forming units and therefore have a Front, two Flank, and a Rear Facing, can perform Supporting Attacks, and so on. Units in skirmish formation never block Line of Sight (remember that this also affects Cover as they can never contribute to Hard Cover).

Units in skirmish formation can only be joined by Characters that have both the same Type and the same Height as the unit. Unless a Character has the exact same base size as all R&F models in the unit, it is considered Mismatched for the purpose of placement within the unit. The unit ceases to be in skirmish formation when all R&F models with Skirmisher are removed as a casualty: immediately contract their skirmish formation into a normal formation, without moving the centre of the first rank. Nudge any unit as normal to maintain base contact if possible.

See figure 40 for an illustration of this rule.

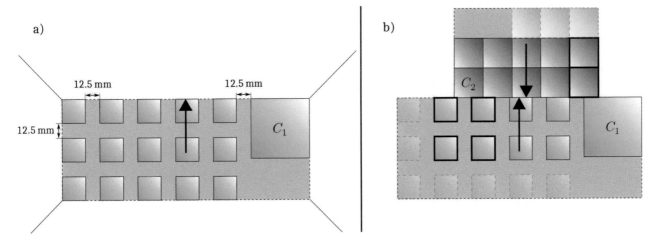

Figure 40: Skirmish formation.

a) An example of a unit in skirmish formation with a joined Mismatching Character.

b) The same unit Engaged in Combat. Models with bold frame can attack a Character (either C_1 or C_2). Models with dashed frame cannot attack at all.

21.A.a.26 Stand Behind

The model can be placed anywhere inside its unit (it doesn't have to be placed as far forwards as possible, even if it has Front Rank). It cannot be placed farther forwards inside a unit than any model with Front Rank but without Stand Behind. Ignore Stand Behind for models with Mismatching Bases.

21.A.a.27 Strider

The model automatically passes Dangerous Terrain Tests caused by Terrain. If more than half of a unit's models have Strider, the unit never loses Steadfast due to Terrain. Sometimes Strider is linked to a specific type of Terrain, stated in brackets. In this case, Strider only applies when interacting with this type of Terrain.

21.A.a.28 Stubborn

A unit with at least one model with Stubborn ignores Discipline modifiers from the Combat Score difference when taking Break Tests or Combat Reform Discipline Tests.

21.A.a.29 Supernal

All attacks made by the model become **Magical Attacks**, including Special Attacks and Crush Attacks. In addition, the model gains **Unstable**, with the following exception: when a unit consisting entirely of models with Supernal loses a combat, it must take a Break Test (Stubborn or Steadfast units ignore Discipline modifiers from the Combat Score difference as normal):

- If the Break Test is passed, ignore all Health Points that would be lost due to Unstable.
- If the Break Test is failed, follow the rules for Unstable as normal.

21.A.a.30 Swift Reform

During the Movement Phase, a unit containing one or more models with Swift Reform may execute a Swift Reform instead of a Reform. The unit makes a Reform with the following exceptions:

- The unit is not prohibited from shooting in the next Shooting Phase (but will still suffer the to-hit modifier for moving and shooting).
- The unit can perform an Advance Move after the Reform. For the purpose of no model being able to end its movement with its centre farther away than its Advance Rate from its starting position, measure this distance after the Reform.
- No model can end its movement (after an Advance Move) with its centre farther away than its March Rate from its starting position before the Reform.

21.A.a.31 Swiftstride

If a unit is composed entirely of models with Swiftstride, its rolls for Charge Range, Flee Distance, Pursuit Distance, and Overrun Distance are subject to Maximised Roll.

21.A.a.32 Tall

Line of Sight drawn to or from a model with Tall is not blocked by models of the same Height (as the model with Tall), unless the intervening model also has Tall. Remember that this also affects Cover (if a model blocks Line of Sight it contributes to Hard Cover, otherwise only to Soft Cover).

21.A.a.33 Terror

The model is immune to the effects of Terror. When a unit with one or more models with Terror declares a Charge, its target must immediately take a Panic Test before declaring its Charge Reaction. If the test is failed, the target of the Charge must declare a Flee Charge Reaction if able to do so.

21.A.a.34 Towering Presence

The model gains **Tall** and can never be joined or join a unit (unless it is a War Platform). A model with Towering Presence increases its Rally Around the Flag and Commanding Presence ranges by 6″.

21.A.a.35 Unbreakable

The model's unit automatically passes all Break Tests. Models with Unbreakable can only join or be joined by models with Unbreakable.

21.A.a.36 Undead

The model gains **Unstable**. Models with Undead cannot perform March Moves, unless their unit starts the March Move within the range of a friendly model's Commanding Presence. The only Charge Reaction a unit with one or more models with Undead can perform is Hold.

When units consisting entirely of models with Undead lose Health Points due to Unstable, the number of lost Health Points can be reduced in certain situations. Apply the modifiers in the following order:

1. If the unit contains at least one model with Stubborn, halve the number of lost Health Points, rounding fractions up.

2. If the unit is Steadfast, ignore any excess Health Point losses above 12.

3. If the unit receives Rally Around the Flag, reduce the number of lost Health Points by the unit's current Rank Bonus. Units without any Rank Bonus reduce the number of lost Health Points by 1 instead.

4. Apply all other modifiers (from Special Items, Model Rules, spells, etc.) afterwards.

21.A.a.37 Unstable

Models with Unstable can only join or be joined by models with Unstable. A unit with one or more models with Unstable does not take a Break Test when losing a Round of Combat, but instead it loses one Health Point for each point of Combat Score difference by which it lost the Round of Combat (with no saves of any kind allowed).

The Health Point losses are allotted in the following order:

1. R&F models, excluding Champions

2. Champion

3. Characters, allotted by the owner of the unit as evenly as possible

21.A.a.38 Vanguard (X)

After Deployment (including Scouting units), models with Vanguard may perform a 12″ move. This move is performed as a combination of Advance Move and/or Reforms, as in the Movement Phase, including any actions and restrictions that normally apply to the unit (e.g. Wheeling, joining units, leaving units, and so on). The 12″ distance is used instead of the unit's Advance Rate and March Rate. In case a figure is stated in brackets, this distance is X″ instead.

This move cannot be used to move within 12″ of enemy units. This is decreased to 6″ for enemy units that have either Scouted or Vanguarded.

If both players have units with Vanguard, alternate moving units one at a time, starting with the player that finished deploying last (note that this is an exception to the rules for Simultaneous Effects). A Combined Unit counts as a single unit for this purpose even if parts of the unit perform separate Vanguard moves (like two Characters Vanguarding out of a Combined Unit). Any game effects that would affect the Combined Unit (such as Banner Enchantments) remain in effect for all parts of the Combined Unit until all parts of the Combined Unit have finished their Vanguard move (even if a Character leaves the unit). Instead of moving a unit, a player may declare to not move any more Vanguarding units.

Units that have moved this way lose Scoring until the end of Game Turn 1 and may not declare Charges in the first Player Turn (if their side has the first turn).

21.A.a.39 War Machine

The model cannot Pursue (which does not prevent it from being affected by Random Movement), declare Charges, or declare Flee Charge Reactions. Characters can never join units with War Machine, and Characters with War Machine cannot join units.

When a War Machine fails a Panic Test, instead of Fleeing it is Shaken until the end of the next Player Turn. War Machines that fail a Break Test are automatically destroyed. War Machines on round bases and units Engaged in Combat with them cannot make Combat Reforms.

When a unit Charges a War Machine on a round base, it can move into base contact by having its Front Facing contact any point of the War Machine's base (it must still maximise the number of models in base contact, see "Contact between Objects", page 11 and figure 31, page 68). No align move is allowed.

When a unit Breaks from Combat and Flees away from a War Machine on a round base, always Pivot the Fleeing unit 180°, so that it's Rear Facing is in contact with the War Machine's base. Otherwise follow the normal rules for units Breaking from Combat and Fleeing.

21.A.a.40 War Platform

Unless selected as a mount for a Character, a model with War Platform gains **Character** with the following exceptions:

- It does not count towards the Characters Army Category (for Army List creation).
- It does not count as Character when Deploying Units (it may still be deployed inside units).
- It cannot issue Duels, accept Duels, or Make Way.
- It can perform Swirling Melee.
- It does not count as Character regarding Bodyguard and Multiple Wounds, unless the War Platform is specifically mentioned in the Bodyguard rule.

The model can join units even if it has Towering Presence, and having Chariot does not prevent it from joining units without Chariot. Additionally, it does not prevent Characters without Chariot from joining a unit containing a model with War Platform and Chariot. When joined to a unit, it must always be placed in the centre of the first rank, possibly pushing back other models with Front Rank, and must keep its position in the centre of the first rank at all times (as long as it is joined to the unit). If two positions are equally central (e.g. in a unit with an even number of models in the first rank and a War Platform replacing an uneven number of models per rank), the War Platform can be placed in either of these positions. If the War Platform cannot be placed in the centre of the the first rank, the model cannot join the unit. A War Platform with Mismatching Base can never join a unit, and only a single War Platform can be in the same unit unless specifically stated otherwise.

21.A.a.41 Wizard Apprentice

The Wizard selects its spells as described in "Spell Selection", page 36.

21.A.a.42 Wizard Adept

The Wizard gains **Channel (1)** and selects its spells as described in "Spell Selection", page 36.

21.A.a.43 Wizard Master

The Wizard gains **Channel (1)** and a +1 modifier to its casting rolls, and selects its spells as described in "Spell Selection", page 36.

21.A.a.44 Wizard Conclave

The Champion of a unit with Wizard Conclave is a **Wizard Adept** and gains +1 Health Point in addition to the normal Attack Value increase associated with being a Champion. This Champion may select up to two spells from predetermined spells given in the unit entry. This overrides the Spell Selection rules for Wizard Adepts.

21.B   Character

Character is a special type of Universal Rule. Unless specifically stated otherwise, any model bought as part of the Characters Army Category of an Army Book has the Character Universal Rule. A model with this rule is referred to as a Character.

All Characters gain the **Front Rank** Universal Rule.

21.B.a   Lone Characters

Characters can operate as a unit consisting of just a single model. In this case, follow the normal rules for units.

21.B.b   Characters Joined to Units

Characters can operate as part of other units, by joining them. This can be done either by deploying the Character in the unit or by moving into contact with the unit during the Movement Phase while performing an Advance Move or a March Move. Units that are Engaged in Combat or Fleeing cannot be joined.

Characters can join other Characters to form a unit consisting only of Characters.

Units that are formed by Characters joining R&F models or other Characters are referred to as Combined Units.

When a Character joins a unit, it must move into a legal position during its Advance or March Move (see "Front Rank", page 95). A Character can choose any legal position it can reach with its move, moving through the unit it joins, possibly displacing other models (including models with Front Rank). Move displaced models as little as possible in order to keep all models in legal positions. If the Character does not have a sufficient movement range to reach a legal position, it cannot join the unit.

When a Character joins a unit with just a single rank, the owner can choose to either displace a model to the second rank, or to expand the unit's width and place the displaced model at either side of the first rank.

When a unit is joined by a Character, the unit cannot move any farther in the same Movement Phase. For determining which model counts as having moved or Marched (e.g. for purposes of shooting), the Character and the unit are treated individually during the Player Turn in which the Character joined the unit. For example, if the unit hasn't moved and the Character has Marched in order to join the unit, the Character counts as having Marched, while the rest of the unit counts as not having moved at all.

Once joined to a unit, the Character is considered as part of the unit for all rules purposes.

21.B.c   R&F Models in a Combined Unit Wiped out

If a Combined Unit has all its R&F models removed as casualties, leaving one or more Characters behind, the remaining Characters will stay a Combined Unit, which is considered to be the same unit for ongoing effects (such as One Turn spells) and Panic (the unit has not been destroyed; the Characters in this Combined Unit may have to take a Panic Test if they have suffered 25% or more casualties). They are treated as a new unit for Rally Tests (i.e. Characters that were part of Fleeing Combined Units at 25% or less of their starting number of Health Points take Rally Tests on their normal Discipline).

21.B.d   Leaving a Combined Unit

A Character can leave a Combined Unit in the Charge Phase and in the Movement Phase if it is able to move (i.e. if it isn't Engaged in Combat, hasn't already moved, isn't Fleeing, etc.). In both cases, any game effects that would affect the Combined Unit (such as Banner Enchantments) remain in effect for all parts of the Combined Unit until the end of the phase (even if a Character leaves the unit), unless specifically stated otherwise (e.g. One Turn spells). The Character ignores models from the Combined Unit for movement purposes and may make a Flying Movement (if it has Fly). Characters leaving a unit do not affect whether or not this unit counts as having moved (e.g. for purposes of shooting).

21.B.d.1 Charging out of a Unit

Declare a Charge with a Character in a Combined Unit (during the Charge Phase as normal) and apply the following rules:

- Use the Character's model for determining Line of Sight and distance to the enemy unit.

- As soon as the Character declares a Charge, it is considered a separate unit (i.e. it uses its own Advance Rate, all hits from Stand and Shoot Charge Reactions will hit the Character, in case of a Flee Charge Reaction the enemy unit Flees away from the Character, etc.).

- Ignore the unit the Character was part of when determining Line of Sight and cover for Stand and Shoot Charge Reactions.

- The unit itself (including other Characters in the unit) cannot declare Charges in the same Player Turn.

- If the Charge is successful, move the Character out of the unit by Charging as normal.

- If the Charge is not successful, the Character makes a Failed Charge Move out of the unit. If the Failed Charge Move is too short to place the Character outside 1″ of the Combined Unit, the Character is no longer considered a separate unit and remains in the Combined Unit. All the models in the Combined Unit are Shaken until the end of the Player Turn.

21.B.d.2   Advance/March Moving out of a Combined Unit

A Character counts as part of the unit until it has physically left it. If a Character does not have enough movement to be placed at least 1″ away from the unit, it cannot leave the unit. A Character cannot leave a unit and rejoin it in the same phase. If one or more Characters want to leave a Combined Unit during the Movement Phase, apply the following rules:

- Choose the Combined Unit and take a single March Test if necessary as per "Moving Units", page 51. The test applies to both Characters and R&F models in the unit, i.e. if the test is failed, none of the models may perform a March Move during this Movement Phase.

- Characters leaving the unit and the remainder of the Combined Unit can perform different types of move (see "Moving Units", page 51).

- Move any Character that can and wishes to leave the unit, then move the remainder of the unit if applicable.

- Once all elements of the chosen Combined Unit that can and wish to have moved, proceed with the next unit.

21.B.e   Distributing Hits onto Combined Units

When a non-Close Combat Attack hits a Combined Unit, there are two possibilities for distributing hits:

Characters are of the same Type –and– same Height –and– there are 5 or more R&F models in the unit	Characters are of a different Type –or– different Height –or– there are 4 or less R&F models in the unit
All hits are distributed onto the R&F Health Pool, Characters cannot suffer any hits.	The player making the attack distributes hits onto the R&F Health Pool and Characters. All simultaneous hits must be distributed as equally as possible, meaning that no model can take a second hit until all models have taken a single hit, and so on.

If a unit of 5 or more R&F models contains several Characters of both the same and different Type or Height, Characters with the same Type and Height as the R&F models are ignored for the hit distributions. Note that hits are never distributed onto Champions.

21.B.f Make Way

At step 3 of the Round of Combat Sequence, any Character placed in the first rank and not in base contact with an enemy model may move into contact with an enemy model. This enemy model must be in base contact with the Character's unit, and it must be attacking the Character's unit in its Front Facing. To perform a Make Way move, the Character switches position with another model (or models) in its unit; these models cannot be Characters. Characters with Mismatching Bases can never perform a Make Way move.

21.C Command Group

Certain units feature the option of upgrading regular models to a Champion, Musician, or Standard Bearer. If so, the model gains the corresponding Model Rule. These models are referred to as a unit's Command Group.

21.C.a Champion

A Champion gains **Front Rank**, **First Amongst Equals**, and **Ordering the Charge**.

21.C.a.1 First Amongst Equals

A Champion gains +1 Attack Value. If it is a Multipart Model, the Attack Value modifier only affects a single model part, which must be a model part without Harnessed or Inanimate.

21.C.a.2 Ordering the Charge

When a unit with a Champion rolls for its Charge Range, it **always** counts as rolling at least a '4'. If the Charge is still failed, ignore this rule and use the rolled dice to determine the Failed Charge Move following the normal rules.

For example, a Charging unit with an Advance Rate of 7″ containing a Champion declares a Charge against an enemy unit that is 11″ away. In case of a Charge Range roll of 2, the Charge will still be successful since the Charge Range roll is considered to be 4, resulting in a Charge Range of 11″.

21.C.a.3 Other Rules Associated with Champions

- Hits from attacks that follow the rules for Distributing Hits are never distributed onto Champions (see page 19).

- When removing non-Champion R&F models as casualties and a Champion is in a position that would normally be removed as a casualty, remove the next eligible R&F model and slide the Champion into the empty spot (see "Removing Casualties", page 81).

- When Raising Health Points, a Champion is the first model that is brought back if it was previously removed as a casualty (see "Raise Health Points", page 60).

- Champions may choose to use a different Shooting Weapon than the other R&F models in their unit (see "Shooting With a Unit", page 61).

- Champions may issue and accept Duels. If a Duel is not accepted, a Champion cannot be chosen as the model that suffers the penalties for refusing a Duel (see "Duels", page 69).

21.C.b Musician

A Musician gains **Swift Reform** and **March to the Beat**.

21.C.b.1 March to the Beat

A unit within 8″ of one or more enemy units that contain a model with March to the Beat suffers −1 Discipline when taking March Tests. Units with at least one model with March to the Beat ignore this modifier.

21.C.c Standard Bearer

A Standard Bearer gains **Combat Bonus**. Certain Standard Bearers may have the option to be upgraded with Banner Enchantments (see "Banner Enchantments", page 116).

21.C.c.1 Combat Bonus

A side with Standard Bearers adds +1 to its Combat Score for each Standard Bearer.

21.C.d   Placing and Moving Command Group Models

Musicians and Standard Bearers can be placed anywhere inside their units.

When making an Advance Move, March Move, or Reform with a unit that includes a Musician and/or a Standard Bearer, these models can be reorganised into a new position as part of the move. This counts towards the distance moved by the unit (measure the distance from the starting position to the ending position of the centre of the Command Group model to determine how far it moved).

Note that Champions are placed and moved inside their units according to the rules in Front Rank as normal.

21.C.e   Removing Command Group Casualties

If a Musician or Standard Bearer is to be removed as a casualty, replace the closest non-Command Group R&F model from the same Health Pool (if there is any) with the Musician or Standard Bearer. The owner chooses if several R&F models are equally close. It is assumed that another soldier picked up their tool and responsibility. Champions are however not replaceable and have their own Health Pool, which can be specifically targeted in certain situations (e.g. by allocating Close Combat Attacks, attacks that target individual models such as attacks from Focused spells, or attacks that target all models in a unit). When a Champion is removed as a casualty, a non-Champion R&F model is moved to fill the empty spot. If enough Health Points are lost from a unit's Health Pool to remove all non-Champion R&F models as casualties, any remaining Health Point losses are allotted to the Champion, even if it is fighting a Duel.

21.D   Personal Protections

If at least one model part has a Personal Protection, the entire Multipart Model follows the rules of the Personal Protection, unless the model's mount is of Gigantic Height (and therefore has the Massive Bulk Universal Rule). In this case, only the mount's Personal Protections are applied.

For example, if a Character with Distracting mounts a horse (Standard Height), the Multipart Model is affected by Distracting. If the Character instead mounts a dragon (Gigantic Height), the Multipart Model is not affected by Distracting.

21.D.a   Conditional Application

Personal Protections may only work against certain attacks, which are then stated in brackets after "against". There may already be some piece of information relative to the rule specified between brackets, as in Aegis (4+). In this case, the conditions for the rule to work are written in the same brackets, after a comma. This can e.g. be certain kinds of attacks or attacks with a given Attack Attribute, like Aegis (4+, against Melee Attacks) or Aegis (2+, against Flaming Attacks).

21.D.b   List of Personal Protections

21.D.b.1 Aegis (X)

Aegis is a Special Save. A model must reroll successful Aegis Saves against Divine Attacks.

21.D.b.2 Cannot be Stomped

For the purposes of Stomp Attacks from enemy models, a model with Cannot be Stomped is never considered to be of Standard Height.

21.D.b.3 Distracting

Close Combat Attacks allocated towards a model with Distracting suffer a –1 to-hit modifier. This to-hit modifier cannot be combined with any other negative to-hit modifiers.

21.D.b.4 Flammable

Flaming Attacks must reroll failed to-wound rolls against a model with Flammable.

21.D.b.5 Fortitude (X)

Fortitude is a Special Save. Fortitude Saves cannot be taken against attacks with Lethal Strike that rolled a natural '6' to wound, or against Flaming Attacks.

21.D.b.6 Hard Target (X)

Shooting Attacks targeting a unit that has more than half of its models with Hard Target (X) suffer a –X to-hit modifier. This rule is cumulative.

21.D.b.7 Parry

Parry can only be used against Close Combat Attacks from the Front Facing. The model gains one of the following effects, whichever would result in a higher Defensive Skill:

- The model gains +1 Defensive Skill.
- The model's Defensive Skill is **always** set to the Offensive Skill of the attacker.

21.E Armour Equipment

There are 2 different types of Armour Equipment. A model can only ever be equipped with one piece of armour of each type, i.e. an optional Suit of Armour replaces a model's default Suit of Armour if applicable. The types of armour below are also referred to as mundane armour:

21.E.a Suits of Armour

- Light Armour: +1 Armour.
- Heavy Armour: +2 Armour.
- Plate Armour: +3 Armour.

21.E.b Shields

- Shield: +1 Armour.

Two-Handed weapons prevent the simultaneous use of a Shield against Melee Attacks (see "Weapons", page 106).

21.F Weapons

Weapons are divided into three categories: Close Combat Weapons, Shooting Weapons, and Artillery Weapons. The weapons listed in the following pages are also referred to as mundane weapons.

21.F.a Close Combat Weapons

Close Combat Weapons are used in close combat and can confer various benefits and drawbacks to the model's Close Combat Attacks. The rules for a Close Combat Weapon are only applied when using the weapon in question (i.e. they don't apply to Special Attacks, such as Stomp Attacks, or when using a different weapon). Mundane Close Combat Weapons are listed in table 9.

21.F.a.1 Choosing a Close Combat Weapon

If a model has more than one Close Combat Weapon, it must choose which one to use in the First Round of Combat, at step 2 of the Round of Combat Sequence. It must then continue to use the same weapon for the duration of that combat. All R&F models in a unit must **always** choose the same Close Combat Weapon, unless they are forced to use enchanted weapons.

Weapon	Rules
Great Weapon	**Two-Handed**. Attacks made with a Great Weapon gain +2 Strength, +2 Armour Penetration, and strike at Initiative Step 0 (regardless of the wielder's Agility).
Halberd	**Two-Handed**. Attacks made with a Halberd gain +1 Strength and +1 Armour Penetration.
Hand Weapon	All models come equipped with a Hand Weapon as their default equipment. If a model has any Close Combat Weapon other than a Hand Weapon, it cannot choose to use the Hand Weapon, unless specifically stated otherwise. Models on foot wielding a Hand Weapon alongside a Shield gain **Parry**.
Lance	Attacks made with a Lance and allocated towards models in the wielders' Front Facing gain **Devastating Charge (+2 Strength, +2 Armour Penetration)**. Infantry cannot use Lances.
Light Lance	Attacks made with a Light Lance and allocated towards models in the wielders' Front Facing gain **Devastating Charge (+1 Strength, +1 Armour Penetration)**. Infantry cannot use Light Lances.
Paired Weapons	**Two-Handed**. The wielder gains +1 Attack Value and +1 Offensive Skill when using Paired Weapons. Attacks made with Paired Weapons ignore Parry (while Paired Weapons are often modelled as two Hand Weapons, they are considered a separate weapon category for rules purposes).
Spear	Attacks made with a Spear gain **Fight in Extra Rank** and +1 Armour Penetration. Attacks made with a Spear gain +2 Agility and an additional +1 Armour Penetration in the First Round of Combat provided the attacking model's unit is not Charging and is not Engaged either in its Flank or Rear Facing. Only Infantry can use Spears.

Table 9: Mundane Close Combat Weapons.

21.F.b Shooting Weapons

Shooting Weapons are used for making Shooting Attacks. Each model part can normally only use one Shooting Weapon per phase even if it is equipped with more than one, and all non-Champion R&F models in a unit must use the same Shooting Weapon. Each Shooting Weapon has a maximum range, a number of shots fired, a Strength, and an Armour Penetration value, and can have one or more Attack Attributes. Attack Attributes listed for a Shooting Weapon only apply to the Shooting Attacks made with that weapon. Mundane Shooting Weapons are listed in table 10.

Weapon	Range	Shots	Strength	Armour Penetration	Attack Attributes
Bow	24"	1	3	0	Volley Fire
Crossbow	30"	1	4	1	Unwieldy
Handgun	24"	1	4	2	Unwieldy
Longbow	30"	1	3	0	Volley Fire
Pistol	12"	1	4	2	Quick to Fire
Throwing Weapons	8"	2	as user	as user	Accurate, Quick to Fire

Table 10: Mundane Shooting Weapons.

21.F.c Artillery Weapons

Artillery Weapons are a special kind of Shooting Weapon. These weapons are often installed on War Machines, but can on other occasions be carried by Chariots or Gigantic Beasts, or contained within Special Items.

Artillery Weapons are Shooting Weapons that always have the **Reload!** Attack Attribute, and they may have specific profiles for range, shots, Strength, Armour Penetration, and other Attack Attributes, which you will find in their description. Some Artillery Weapons may have further rules as detailed below.

21.F.c.1 Cannon

Cannon attacks ignore to-hit modifiers from Soft Cover and Hard Cover. They gain a +1 to-hit modifier when targeting units consisting entirely of models of Gigantic Height that do not benefit from Cover. On a natural to-hit roll of '1' a Cannon Misfires: roll on the Misfire Table (table 11, page 109) and apply the corresponding result (a to-hit roll resulting in a Misfire cannot be rerolled).

21.F.c.2 Catapult (X×Y)

Catapult attacks ignore to-hit modifiers from Soft Cover and Hard Cover. Resolve Catapult attacks as follows:

- On a natural to-hit roll of '1', it Misfires: roll on the Misfire Table (table 11, page 109) and apply the corresponding result (a to-hit roll resulting in a Misfire cannot be rerolled).

- On a successful to-hit roll, the attack gains Area Attack (X×Y). Resolve the attack with the Strength and Armour Penetration stated in the Catapult's description.

- On any other to-hit result, roll to hit with a new Catapult attack, referred to as Partial Hit, and ignore any Misfire. If it hits, this attack gains Area Attack (X×Y), but you reduce both X and Y by 1. If either value reaches 0, no hits are inflicted. All hits are at half Strength and half Armour Penetration, rounding fractions up. In addition, the attack loses all benefits from the Strength, Armour Penetration, and/or Attack Attributes written in square brackets (if any; see Area Attack). If it misses, no further attack can be generated this way.

21.F.c.3 Flamethrower

Flamethrowers do not roll to hit. Instead, roll a D6 (this is not considered a to-hit roll). On a natural roll of '1', it Misfires: roll on the Misfire Table (table 11, page 109) with a −1 modifier and apply the corresponding result. On any other natural result the attack is successful. Determine which Arc of the target the attacker is Located in:

- If the attacker is Located in the Front or the Rear Arc, the attack causes D6 hits, +D3 hits for each rank after the first up to a maximum of +4D3.

- If the attacker is Located in either Flank Arc, the attack causes D6 hits, +D3 hits for each file after the first up to a maximum of +4D3.

The total number of hits cannot exceed the number of models in the unit.

Some Flamethrowers have a higher Strength, Armour Penetration, and/or additional Attack Attributes stated in curly brackets (such as Strength 4 {5}, Armour Penetration 1 {2}, {Multiple Wounds (D3)}). If so, use the Strength, Armour Penetration, and Attack Attributes in curly brackets when shooting at a target within Short Range.

21.F.c.4 Volley Gun

The number of shots fired by a Volley Gun is a random number. When rolling for the number of shots for a Volley Gun attack, if a single natural '6' is rolled (after any reroll), this attack suffers a −1 to-hit modifier; instead, if two or more natural '6' are rolled, the attack fails and the Volley Gun Misfires: roll on the Misfire Table (table 11, page 109) and apply the corresponding result.

21.F.d The Misfire Table

A to-hit roll resulting in a Misfire cannot be rerolled. When an Artillery Weapon Misfires, roll a D6 and consult table 11 below (a result of '0' or less may happen when there is a negative modifier to the roll, as for Flamethrowers).

Result	Misfire Effect
0 **(or less)**	**Explosion!** All models within D6″ of the Misfiring model suffer a hit with Strength 5 and Armour Penetration 2. The shooting model is then destroyed and removed as a casualty.
1–2	**Breakdown** The model cannot shoot with the weapon for the rest of the game.
3–4	**Jammed** The Artillery Weapon may not shoot in the owner's next Player Turn. If the model is a War Machine, the model is Shaken until the end of the owner's next Player Turn instead.
5+	**Malfunction** The shooting model loses a Health Point with no saves of any kind allowed.

Table 11: Misfire Table.

21.G Attack Attributes

Attack Attributes can be given to a model part, to a weapon, to a spell, or to a Special Attack. Remember that an Attack Attribute that is given to a unit is automatically given to every model in that unit (see "Units", page 8), and if it is given to a model, it is automatically given to all model parts of that model (see "Multipart Models", page 7).

Attack Attributes given to a weapon, spell, or Special Attack are always applied to the attacks made with that weapon, spell, or Special Attack. They are however not applied to any other attacks made by the corresponding model part.

Example: A Character on a Chariot has a a Weapon Enchantment that makes the attacks made with its Hand Weapon Divine Attacks and Magical Attacks. This means that only the Close Combat Attacks made with the enchanted weapon become Divine Attacks and Magical Attacks, while all other attacks made by the model (e.g. Impact Hits and Close Combat Attacks from the horses pulling the Chariot) are not affected.

Attack Attributes are divided into the following sub-categories that define what attacks they affect when given to a model part. Note that these sub-categories are irrelevant for Attack Attributes given to a weapon, spell, or an attack, including Special Attacks (so an Attack Attribute with the Close Combat keyword can be given e.g. to a Shooting Weapon).

Close Combat

A model part with an Attack Attribute with this keyword applies the rules of the Attack Attribute to all its Close Combat Attacks.

Shooting

A model part with an Attack Attribute with this keyword applies the rules of the Attack Attribute to all its Shooting Attacks that are not Special Attacks.

Example: A unit is the target of a spell that makes the unit's attacks Divine Attacks and Flaming Attacks. Divine Attacks has the keyword Close Combat, while Flaming Attacks has the keywords Close Combat and Shooting. This means that the Close Combat Attacks of all model parts of that unit are now both Divine Attacks and Flaming Attacks, while the Shooting Attacks of all model parts of the unit are only Flaming Attacks. Any Special Attacks (including Special Attacks that are Shooting Attacks) or spells from the unit are not affected.

21.G.a Conditional Application

Attack Attributes may only work against certain enemies, which are then stated in brackets after "against". There may already be some piece of information relative to the rule specified between brackets, as in Multiple Wounds (2). In this case the conditions for the rule to work are written in the same brackets, after a comma. This can e.g. be all models from a given Army Book, with a given Model Rule, of a given Height, or of a given Type.

If the Attack Attribute is effective against more than one type of enemy, they are separated by commas. If no comma but instead "and" is used, this means that the rule works only against enemies that fulfil all criteria. For example, Multiple Wounds (2, against Large and Beasts, Gigantic) means that Multiple Wounds can be used against models that are both Large and Beasts, as well as against models that are Gigantic, regardless of the models' Type.

Attack Attributes with Conditional Application can only be applied when the affected attacks are either allocated towards or distributed onto a Health Pool where all models fulfil the requirements.

21.G.b List of Attack Attributes

21.G.b.1 Accurate – Shooting

The attack doesn't suffer the −1 to-hit modifier for shooting at Long Range.

21.G.b.2 Area Attack (X×Y)

When the attack hits, determine the position of the attacker's base:

- In case of a Ranged Attack, determine which Arc of the target the attacker's base is Located in.

- In case of a Melee Attack, determine which Facing of the target the attacker is Engaged in.

Front or Rear: Choose up to Y different ranks of the target.
Flank: Choose up to Y different files of the target.

For each rank/file selected this way, the unit suffers X hits, to a maximum equal to the number of models in this rank/file. A single Area Attack can never cause more hits than there are models in the unit.

Some Area Attacks have a higher Strength, Armour Penetration, and/or additional Attack Attributes stated in square brackets (e.g. Strength 3 [7], Armour Penetration 0 [4], [Multiple Wounds (D3)]). If so, a single hit from this attack, chosen by the attacker (following the normal rules for Distributing Hits), uses the Strength, Armour Penetration, and Attack Attributes in brackets. The bracketed values and Attack Attributes are not applied to any other hits.

Figure 41 illustrates examples of different Area Attacks.

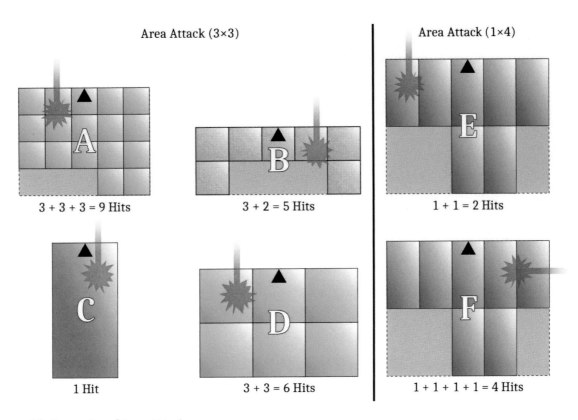

Figure 41: Examples of Area Attacks.

Units A to D are hit by an Area Attack (3×3) from an attacker Located in their Front Arc.

In unit A, there are 3 ranks with more than 3 models. Number of hits: 3 + 3 + 3 = 9.

In unit B, the first rank has more than 3 models, but the second rank only has two models. There is no third rank. Number of hits: 3 + 2 = 5.

Since unit C is a single model, there will always only be a single rank with a single model. Number of hits: 1.

In unit D, the first and second rank have 3 models. There is no third rank. Number of hits: 3 + 3 = 6.

Unit E is hit by an Area Attack (1×4) from an attacker Located in its Front Arc. The first and second rank have more than 1 model. There is no third or fourth rank. Number of hits: 1 + 1 = 2.

Unit F is hit by an Area Attack (1×4) from an attacker Located in its Flank Arc. There are more than 4 files with 1 or more models. Number of hits: 1 + 1 + 1 + 1 = 4.

21.G.b.3 Battle Focus – Close Combat

If the attack hits with a natural to-hit roll of '6', the attack causes one additional hit (i.e. usually two hits instead of one).

In order for Shooting Attacks using Hopeless Shots to cause one additional hit, the first to-hit roll must be a natural '6' and the second to-hit roll must be successful in order to hit the target.

21.G.b.4   Crush Attack – Close Combat

At the end of step 4 of the Round of Combat Sequence (just after issuing and accepting Duels), the model part may declare that it will use its Crush Attack this Round of Combat. It performs a single Close Combat Attack at Initiative Step 0, with Strength 10, Armour Penetration 10 (regardless of the user's Agility, Strength, and Armour Penetration), and Multiple Wounds (D3+1). The following restrictions apply to Crush Attacks:

· They cannot be made as Supporting Attacks.

· They never benefit from any weapons or other Attack Attributes the model part may have.

· The model part cannot make any other Close Combat Attacks during this Round of Combat (including other Crush Attacks, but can still use its Special Attacks such as Stomp Attacks or Impact Hits).

21.G.b.5 Devastating Charge (X)

A Charging model part with Devastating Charge, or using a weapon with Devastating Charge, gains the Model Rules and Characteristic modifiers stated in brackets.

For example, a model part with Devastating Charge (+1 Strength, Poison Attacks) gains +1 Strength and Poison Attacks when it is Charging.

Remember that Special Attacks cannot be affected by Attack Attributes, so the Model Rules and Characteristic modifiers gained from Devastating Charge are not applied to Special Attacks, like Impact Hits and Stomp Attacks, unless specifically stated otherwise.

This rule is cumulative: a model part with several instances of Devastating Charge applies all Attack Attributes and Characteristic modifiers from all of them when Charging.

21.G.b.6 Divine Attacks – Close Combat

Successful Aegis Saves taken against the attack must be rerolled.

21.G.b.7 Fight in Extra Rank – Close Combat

Model parts with Fight in Extra Rank, or using a weapon with Fight in Extra Rank, can make Supporting Attacks from an additional rank (normally, this means that models with Fight in Extra Rank will be able to make Supporting Attacks from the third rank). This rule is cumulative, allowing an additional rank to make Supporting Attacks for each instance of Fight in Extra Rank.

21.G.b.8 Flaming Attacks – Close Combat, Shooting

The attack ignores Fortitude Saves and must reroll failed to-wound rolls against models with Flammable.

21.G.b.9 Harnessed – Close Combat

Model parts with Harnessed cannot make Supporting Attacks and cannot use weapons. Shooting Weapons carried by model parts with Harnessed can be used by other model parts of the same model (as long as they do not have Harnessed or Inanimate). A model with at least one model part with Harnessed is considered to be mounted.

21.G.b.10 Hatred – Close Combat

During the First Round of Combat, failed to-hit rolls from attacks with Hatred must be rerolled.

21.G.b.11 Inanimate – Close Combat

Model parts with Inanimate cannot make Close Combat Attacks and cannot use Shooting Weapons. Shooting Weapons carried by model parts with Inanimate can be used by other model parts of the same model (as long as they do not have Harnessed or Inanimate).

21.G.b.12 Lethal Strike – Close Combat

An attack with Lethal Strike that wounds with a natural to-wound roll of '6' has its Armour Penetration **set** to 10 and ignores Fortitude Saves.

21.G.b.13 Lightning Reflexes – Close Combat

A Close Combat Attack with Lightning Reflexes gains a +1 to-hit modifier. Model parts with this Attack Attribute wielding Great Weapons do not gain this +1 to-hit modifier, but strike with the Great Weapon at the Initiative Step corresponding to their Agility instead of always striking at Initiative Step 0.

21.G.b.14 Magical Attacks – Close Combat, Shooting

The Attack Attribute doesn't confer any additional effects. However, the Attack Attribute interacts with other rules, such as Aegis (X, against Magical Attacks).

21.G.b.15 March and Shoot – Shooting

March Moving in the same Player Turn does not prevent the attack from being performed, unless the attack is also subject to Move or Fire.

21.G.b.16 Move or Fire – Shooting

The attack may not be used if the attacking model has made an Advance Move, March Move, Random Movement, Reform, or Pivot during the current Player Turn. Note that the normal limitations still apply (e.g. no shooting after a Failed Charge Move).

21.G.b.17 Multiple Wounds (X) – Close Combat

Unsaved wounds caused by the attacks are multiplied into the value given in brackets (X). If the value is a dice (e.g. Multiple Wounds (D3)), roll one dice for each unsaved wound from an attack with Multiple Wounds. The amount of wounds that the attack is multiplied into can never be higher than the Health Points Characteristic of the target (excluding Health Points lost previously in the battle).

For example, if a Multiple Wounds (D6) attack wounds a unit of Trolls (HP 3) and rolls a '5' for the multiplier, the number of unsaved wounds is reduced to 3, even if the Troll unit has already lost one or two Health Points previously in battle.

If Clipped Wings is stated after the X value in brackets, any unsaved wound caused by the attack against a model with Fly is multiplied into X+1 instead of X.

21.G.b.18 Poison Attacks – Close Combat, Shooting

If the attack hits with a natural to-hit roll of '6', it automatically wounds with no to-wound roll needed.

Shooting Attacks using Hopeless Shot automatically wound only if the first to-hit roll is a natural '6'. Note that the second to-hit roll must still be successful in order to hit the target.

If the attack can be turned into more than one hit (e.g. a hit with Area Attack or Battle Focus), only a single hit, chosen by the attacker, automatically wounds. All other hits must roll to wound as normal.

21.G.b.19 Quick to Fire – Shooting

The attack doesn't suffer the −1 to-hit modifier for Moving and Shooting.

21.G.b.20 Reload! – Shooting

The attack cannot be used for a Stand and Shoot Charge Reaction.

21.G.b.21 Toxic Attacks – Close Combat

The attack has its Strength **always** set to 3 and its Armour Penetration **always** set to 10.

21.G.b.22 Two-Handed

A model using a weapon with Two-Handed cannot simultaneously use a Shield against Melee Attacks.

21.G.b.23 Unwieldy – Shooting

The attack suffers an additional –1 to-hit modifier for Moving and Shooting (for a total of –2). When combined with Quick to Fire, the attack can only ignore the normal –1 to-hit modifier for Moving and Shooting, not the additional –1 to-hit modifier from Unwieldy.

21.G.b.24 Volley Fire – Shooting

If at least one model in a unit can draw Line of Sight to the target, then all model parts using Volley Fire in the same unit ignore all intervening models of their own Height or smaller for Line of Sight and Cover purposes.

In addition, unless making a Stand and Shoot Charge Reaction, models in a unit in Line Formation that has not moved during this Player Turn may shoot from one additional rank (usually this means that they can shoot from the first three ranks).

21.G.b.25 Weapon Master – Close Combat

At the beginning of each Round of Combat, model parts with Weapon Master may choose which weapon they fight with. This includes selecting to use a Hand Weapon even if they have other weapons. If armed with a weapon with a Weapon Enchantment, the model part must still use it.

21.H   Special Attacks

A model part with Special Attacks can make a special type of attack specified by the corresponding rules. Attacks made using Special Attacks cannot be affected by weapons or Attack Attributes, unless specifically stated otherwise.

21.H.a   List of Special Attacks

21.H.a.1   Breath Attack (X)

A model part with Breath Attack can use it only once during the game. If a model has more than one Breath Attack, it can only use one Breath Attack in a single phase. It can be used either as a Shooting Attack or as a Special Attack when Engaged in Combat.

- As a Shooting Attack with **March and Shoot**: choose a target using the normal rules for Shooting Attacks (it can be used for a Stand and Shoot Charge Reaction). The attack has a range of 6″. A model part with both a Breath Attack and a Shooting Weapon can use both in the same Shooting Phase, however only against the same target.

- As a Special Attack when Engaged in Combat: the attack is made at the model part's Agility. Declare that you are using the Breath Attack at the start of the Initiative Step (before rolling to hit), and choose a unit in base contact as a target.

No matter if it is used as a Shooting or Melee Attack, the target of the Breath Attack suffers 2D6 hits. The Strength, Armour Penetration, and Attack Attributes (if any) of these hits are given within brackets, such as in Breath Attack (Str 4, AP 1, Flaming Attacks). If several models in the same unit have this Special Attack, roll for the number of hits separately for each model.

21.H.a.2 Grind Attacks (X)

A model part with Grind Attacks resolves these attacks at its Agility. It must choose an enemy unit in base contact with it. The chosen enemy unit suffers a number of hits equal to the value stated in brackets (X). These hits are resolved with the model part's Strength and Armour Penetration.

If a model has both Grind Attacks and Impact Hits, it may only use one of these rules in the same Round of Combat (the owner may choose which). If several model parts in a unit have Grind Attacks and if X is a random number (e.g. Grind Attacks (2D3)), roll for the number of hits separately for each model part.

21.H.a.3 Impact Hits (X)

At Initiative Step 10, a Charging model part with Impact Hits must choose an enemy unit that is in base contact with the attacking model's Front Facing. This unit suffers a number of hits equal to the value stated in brackets (X). These hits are resolved with the attacking model part's Strength and Armour Penetration.

If a model has both Grind Attacks and Impact Hits, it may only use one of these rules in the same Round of Combat (the owner may choose which). In case of Multipart Models, only model parts that also have Harnessed or Inanimate can use Impact Hits. If several models in a unit have Impact Hits, and if X is a random number (e.g. Impact Hits (D6)), roll for the number of hits separately for each model part.

21.H.a.4 Stomp Attacks (X)

At Initiative Step 0, a model part with Stomp Attacks must choose an enemy model of Standard Height in base contact with it. The chosen model's unit suffers a number of hits equal to the value stated in brackets (X). These hits can only be distributed onto models of Standard Height (ignore models of a different Height when distributing hits). They are resolved with the model part's Strength and Armour Penetration.

In case of Multipart Models, only model parts that also have Harnessed can use Stomp Attacks. If several models in a unit have this Special Attack, and if X is a random number (e.g. Stomp Attacks (D6)), roll for the number of hits separately for each model part.

21.H.a.5 Sweeping Attack

This attack may be used by units containing models with Sweeping Attack. When the unit Advance Moves or March Moves, you may nominate a single unengaged enemy unit that the unit with Sweeping Attack moved through or over during this move (meaning their Unit Boundaries were overlapping, even partially). The whole unit makes the Sweeping Attack against the nominated enemy unit, which is resolved when the March or Advance Move is completed. Follow the description in the unit entry. These attacks hit automatically and count as ranged Special Attacks. Each Sweeping Attack can only be performed once per Player Turn.

22 Special Items

When building their armies, players have the option to individually upgrade the mundane equipment of certain models, usually Characters and Standard Bearers, by buying Special Items for these models. Some Special Items are shared by most armies of T9A (they can be found in The 9ᵗʰ Age: Fantasy Battles – Arcane Compendium), while army-specific Special Items can be found in the corresponding Army Books.

All Special Items are **One of a Kind** unless specifically stated otherwise.

22.A   Special Item Categories

All Special Items belong to one of the following categories:

- Weapon Enchantments
- Armour Enchantments
- Banner Enchantments
- Artefacts

Each category of Special Items is subject to the rules below.

22.A.a   Weapon Enchantments

Weapon Enchantments are upgrades to weapons. The upgraded mundane weapon is referred to as enchanted weapon and follows all rules for both the original weapon and the Weapon Enchantment. The following rules apply to Weapon Enchantments and enchanted weapons:

- A model may only have a single Weapon Enchantment.
- If a model has more than one weapon, it must be noted on the Army List which weapon has been enchanted (remember that all models are equipped with a Hand Weapon).
- Each Weapon Enchantment applies to a specific weapon (e.g. a Great Weapon) or a category of weapons (e.g. Close Combat Weapons). Note that Shooting Weapons that count as a Close Combat Weapon in close combat (such as a Brace of Pistols from the Empire of Sonnstahl Army Book) cannot normally be Enchanted with a Close Combat Weapon enchantment.
- A model armed with an enchanted weapon (including a Hand Weapon) must use it.

22.A.b   Armour Enchantments

Armour Enchantments are upgrades to Armour Equipment. The upgraded mundane armour is referred to as enchanted armour and follows all rules for both the original Armour Equipment and the Armour Enchantment. The following rules apply to Armour Enchantments and enchanted armour:

- Each piece of armour a model is carrying may be enchanted with a single Armour Enchantment.
- If the wearer has more than one piece of armour that could be enchanted, it must be noted on the Army List which one has been enchanted. If a model has no Armour Equipment, it cannot take Armour Enchantments.
- Each Armour Enchantment applies to a specific piece of armour (e.g. Heavy Armour) or a category of armour (e.g. Suits of Armour).

22.A.c   Banner Enchantments

Banner Enchantments are upgrades to Standard Bearers and Battle Standard Bearers. The upgraded banner is referred to as enchanted banner. Each banner may normally only have a single Banner Enchantment, except for Battle Standard Bearers, who may take up to two Banner Enchantments.

22.A.d Artefacts

A model may have up to two Artefacts.

22.B Properties of Special Items

22.B.a Dominant

A model may only have a single Dominant Special Item.

22.B.b Who is Affected

Special Items may affect different targets:

- The wielder, wearer, or bearer: these terms mean the same thing for rules purposes and refer to the model part the Special Item was bought for (and don't affect its mount).
- Models, the wearer's model, or the bearer's model: these terms refer to all model parts of the models, including their mounts (note that these terms override the Massive Bulk rules).
- Units, the wearer's unit, or the bearer's unit: this type of Special Item affects all model parts in the target unit or in the same unit as the wearer/bearer of the Special Item (including mounts and the wearer/bearer itself).

22.B.c One Use Only

These effects can only be used once per game.

23 Summaries

This chapter is designed as a summary of the Rulebook that you can print out separately and keep at the table when playing, providing easy access to overviews and summaries of the most important rules. However, it does not replace the Rulebook. In situations where the summaries are unclear, please refer to the corresponding Rulebook chapters – the Rulebook always overrules the summaries.

eneral

rn

standard game lasts for 6 **Game Turns**, each divided o two **Player Turns**. Each Player Turn is divided into e phases, performed in the following order:

1 Charge Phase
2 Movement Phase
3 Magic Phase
4 Shooting Phase
5 Melee Phase

Priority of Modifiers

Priority Step	Modifier
1	Values **set** to a certain number and values **set** to another model's value. If the other model's Characteristic is modified, apply these modifiers before setting the Characteristic.
2	Multiplication and division. Round fractions up.
3	Addition and subtraction.
4	Rolls **always** or **never** succeeding or failing on certain results, and Characteristics **always** or **never** set to a certain value or range of values.

When several modifiers within a group are to be applied to a value or dice roll, apply them in the order that results in the lowest value or success chance of the dice roll.

odel Type and Height – related Model Rules

Infantry	Beast	Cavalry	Construct
None	Swiftstride	Cannot be Stomped Swiftstride Tall	Cannot use Stomp Attacks Chariot

	Standard	Large	Gigantic
Model Rules	None	Stomp Attacks (1)	Fear Massive Bulk Stomp Attacks (D6) Terror Towering Presence
Full Ranks	5	3	1
Supporting Attacks	1	3	5

re-Game

re-Game Sequence

1 Decide on the size of the game
2 Share your Army List with your opponent
3 Build the Battlefield
4 Determine the Deployment Type
5 Determine the Secondary Objective
6 Determine the Deployment Zones
7 Select Spells
8 Declare Special Deployment (Ambush, Scout)
9 Deployment Phase

eployment Phase Sequence

1 Determine who deploys first
2 Take turns deploying units
3 Declare intent to go first or second
4 Deploy remaining units
5 Deploy Scouting units (starting with the player who finished deploying first)
6 Move Vanguarding units (starting with the player who finished deploying last)
7 Other rules and abilities
8 Roll for first turn

Deployment Types

1 – Frontline Clash
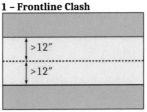

2 – Dawn Assault
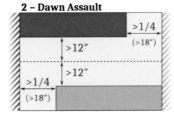

3 – Counterthrust
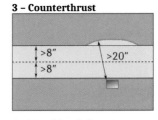

4 – Encircle
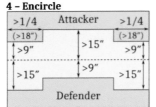

5 – Refused Flank
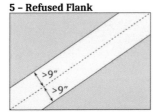

6 – Marching Columns
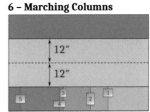

The player who chooses the Deployment Zone also chooses the short Board Edges for 2, who is the attacker for 4, and the diagonal for 5. This player also starts choosing or placing in 4, 5, and 6.

2 – Dawn Assault: Players may choose up to two units as Ambushers coming from their short Board Edge.

3 – Counterthrust: Players must only deploy a single non-Character unit during their first 3 turns. Units must be deployed at least 20" away from enemies.

6 – Marching Columns: Players must only deploy a single non-Character unit during their first 3 turns. Each unit must be closer to the short Board Edge chosen by the owner than the previous friendly units (War Machines, War Platforms, Characters, and Scouts ignore this). Possibility to make units Delayed.

condary Objectives

- Hold the Ground
ave more Scoring Units than your opponent within of the centre of the board at the end of a Game Turn her than the first) to gain a counter.

- King of the Hill
er Spell Selection, each player chooses a non-passable Terrain Feature not entirely in their De-yment Zone. At the end of the game, have Scoring its inside your opponent's Terrain Feature.

2 – Breakthrough
Be the player with the most Scoring Units inside their opponent's Deployment Zone at the end of the game (up to 3).

5 – Capture the Flags
Destroy more Scoring Units than your opponent. Each player must have at least 3 Scoring Units; else, the opponent marks non-Scoring Units to destroy.

3 – Spoils of War
Three markers on the Centre Line that can be picked up by Scoring Units by being in contact with them at the beginning of their Player Turn. At the end of the game, be the player with the most units carrying markers.

6 – Secure Target
Both players place a marker more than 12" from their Deployment Zones and 24" away from the other marker. Control a marker by having more Scoring Units within 6" of it. Be the player controlling most markers at the end of the game.

Charge Phase

Charge Phase Sequence

1	Start of the Charge Phase (and start of the Player Turn)
2	The Active Player chooses a unit and declares a Charge
3	The Reactive Player declares and resolves their Charge Reaction
4	Repeat steps 2–3 of this sequence until all units that wish to declare a Charge have done so
5	The Active Player chooses a unit that declared a Charge, then rolls for Charge Range, and moves the unit
6	Repeat step 5 of this sequence until all units that declared a Charge have moved
7	End of the Charge Phase

Maximising Contact

Charge Moves must be made so the following conditions are satisfied as best as possible, decreasing priority order.

- 1st priority: Make contact with no enemy units other than the one that was Charg[ed]. If it will be unavoidable to make contact with more than one enemy unit, make cont[act] with as few enemy units as possible. Follow the rules for Multiple Charges.

- 2nd priority: Maximise the total number of Charging units that make contact (n[ote] that this is only applicable when multiple units Charge the same unit).

- 3rd priority: Avoid rotating the Charged unit. If it is unavoidable, rotate the unit [as] little as possible. Remember that units Engaged in Combat cannot be rotated.

- 4th priority: Maximise the number of models (on both sides) in base contact wit[h at] least one enemy model (including models fighting across gaps).

Movement Phase

Movement Phase Sequence

1	Start of the Movement Phase
2	Rally Fleeing units and perform any Flee Moves
3	Select one of your units and a type of move (Advance, March, Reform), then move the unit
4	Repeat step 3, each time choosing a new unit that has not yet moved in the Movement Phase
5	End of the Movement Phase

Chances to Pass a Charge Range Roll

Probabilities (in percentage) to pass a Charge Range roll depending on the remainin[g] distance (i.e. the total distance minus the Advance Rate Characteristic):

	2	3	4	5	6	7	8	9	10	11	12
Charge	100	97	92	83	72	58	42	28	17	8	3
Charge + Swiftstride	100	99	98	95	89	81	68	52	36	20	7
Charge + reroll	100	99	99	97	92	83	66	48	31	16	5
Charge + Swiftstride + reroll	100	99	99	99	99	96	90	77	59	36	14

Terrain

Dangerous Terrain Tests

Dangerous Terrain (DT) Test during March, Charge, Failed Charge, Flee, Pursuit, or Overrun Moves. 1 hit with Armour Penetration 10 that wounds automatically [on] each failed roll.

	Standard	Large	Gigantic	Chariot
Number of D6 rolled	1	2	3	+1

	Infantry	Beast	Cavalry	Construct	Notes
Forests			DT (1)	DT (1)	DT (1) for Flying Movement
Ruins	DT (1)*	DT (1)*	DT (2)*	DT (2)*	*Unless Skirmisher
Water Terrain	DT (1)*	DT (1)*			*Standard Height and on foot only
Walls				DT (2)	

Other Terrain Rules

Cover and Line of Sight rules described in Shooting Phase.

	Rules (not including Cover and Line of Sight)
Fields	None
Forests	No Steadfast Infantry with Light Troops are Stubborn (unless Towering Presence or Fly)
Hills	Reroll failed Charge Range rolls when Charging from a Hill
Impassable Terrain	Models cannot move into or through
Ruins	None
Walls	Units with Front Facing in contact gain Distracting against Charging enemies
Water Terrain	No Steadfast Lose Flaming Attacks when attacking from or into it with Melee Attacks

Magic Phase

Magic Phase Sequence

1. Start of the Magic Phase
2. Draw a Flux Card
3. Siphon the Veil
4. Cast a spell with one of your models (see "Spell Casting Sequence")
5. Repeat step 4 for each spell the Active Player wishes to cast
6. End of the Magic Phase

Spell Casting Sequence

A	Casting Attempt. If failed, skip steps B–F
B	Dispelling Attempt. If successful, skip steps C–F
C	In case of Broken Concentration, skip steps D–E and go directly to step F
D	Resolve the spell effect
E	If applicable, choose target(s) for the Attribute Spell and resolve its effect
F	If applicable, apply the Miscast effect

Casting Attempt

1. The Active Player declares which Wizard is casting which spell and how many Magic Dice will be used. If applicable, they also declare which version of the spell is used and what its targets are. Between 1 and 5 dice from the Active Player's Magic Dice pool must be used.
2. The Active Player rolls the chosen number of Magic Dice from the Magic Dice pool and adds the results of the rolled dice and any Casting Modifiers together. This total is referred to as the total casting roll.
3. The Casting Attempt is passed if the total casting roll is **equal to or greater** than the spell's Casting Value. The Casting Attempt fails if the total casting roll is less than the spell's Casting Value. Note that the Casting Attempt may Fizzle if 2 or more dice were used (see "Fizzle").

Dispelling Attempt

1. The Reactive Player declares how many Magic Dice will be used from their pool. The Reactive Player must use at least 1 dice for a Dispelling Attempt. Note that there is no maximum number of Magic Dice allowed to be used for a Dispelling Attempt.
2. The Reactive Player rolls the chosen number of dice and adds the results of the rolled dice and any Dispelling Modifiers together, to get the total dispelling roll.
3. The Dispelling Attempt is successful if the total dispelling roll is **equal to or greater** than the total casting roll. If so, the spell is dispelled and the spell is not cast. The Dispelling Attempt fails if the total dispelling roll is less than the total casting roll. If so, the spell is successfully cast. Note that the Dispelling Attempt may Fizzle if 2 or more dice were used (see "Fizzle").

Bound Spell Casting Attempt

1. The Active Player declares which model will cast which Bound Spell, and whether they will use 2 or 3 Magic Dice. If applicable, the Active Player also declares the targets of the spell. The spell is always cast with the basic version as Bound Spells cannot be Boosted.
2. The Active Player removes the chosen number of Magic Dice (2 or 3) from their Magic Dice pool (do not roll them).
3. The Casting Attempt is always passed.

Fizzle

When a Casting Attempt or Dispelling Attempt is failed for which 2 dice or more are used, any Magic Dice that rolled a natural '1' are returned to the Magic Dice pool they were taken from. Note that this does not apply to passed Casting Attempts that are then dispelled.

Flux Cards

Flux Card	1	2	3	4	5	6	7	8
Magic Dice	4	5	5	5	5	6	6	7
Veil Tokens	3	2	5	7	9	5	7	7
Miscast Modifiers	+1							-1

Miscast

Three of a kind:	**Miscast Effects** (after resolving the spell and Attribute effects, unless 111)
000 or lower	No effect.
111	**Broken Concentration**
	The Casting Attempt fails (apply Fizzle as normal).
222	**Witchfire**
	The Caster's unit suffers **1D6 hits** with Armour Penetration 2, Magical Attacks, and a Strength equal to the number of Magic Dice that were used for the casting roll.
333	**Magical Inferno**
	The Caster's unit suffers **2D6 hits** with Armour Penetration 2, Magical Attacks, and a Strength equal to the number of Magic Dice that were used for the casting roll.
444	**Amnesia**
	The Caster cannot cast the Miscast spell anymore this game.
555	**Backlash**
	The Caster suffers **2 hits** that wound on 4+ with Armour Penetration 10 and Magical Attacks.
666	**Implosion**
	The Caster suffers **4 hits** that wound on 4+ with Armour Penetration 10 and Magical Attacks.
777 or higher	**Breach in the Veil**
	The Caster's model is removed as a casualty (no saves of any kind allowed).

Shooting Phase

Shooting Phase Sequence

1	Start of the Shooting Phase
2	Select one of your units and perform a Shooting Attack
3	Repeat step 2 with a different unit that has not performed a Shooting Attack during this phase yet
4	When all units that can (and want to) shoot have done so, the Shooting Phase ends

To-Hit Modifiers

Long Range	−1	Stand and Shoot	−1
(if Accurate)	0	Soft Cover	−1
Moving and Shooting	−1	Hard Cover	−2
(if Quick to Fire)	0	Hard Target (X)	−X
(if Unwieldy)	−2		
(if both)	−1		

Line of Sight and Cover

Determine Line of Sight, range, and Cover for each shooting model. A model is considered to have Line of Sight to a unit if it can draw Line of Sight (in the unit's Front Arc) to any part of the other unit's Unit Boundary.

Choose a point on the shooting model's Front Facing. From the chosen point, check how large the fraction of the Target Facing is that is behind obstructions. If half or more of the Target Facing is obscured, the target benefits from Cover.

Models always ignore their own unit and the Terrain Feature they are inside for Cover purposes.

Selection of Shooting Rules

Each unit can only shoot once per phase. All models in the same unit must shoot at the same target. Only models in the first and second rank may shoot. All Rank models except Champions must use the same type of Shooting Attack. In case of Multipart Models, each model part can make a Shooting Attack in the same phase.

Hopeless Shots: In order to hit on 7+, hit on 6+ and then roll 4+.

Misfire Table for Artillery Weapons

Result	Misfire Effect
0 (or less)	**Explosion!** All models within D6″ of the Misfiring model suffer a hit with Strength 5 and Armour Penetration 2. The shooting model is then destroyed and removed as a casualty.
1–2	**Breakdown** The model cannot shoot with the weapon for the rest of the game.
3–4	**Jammed** The Artillery Weapon may not shoot in the owner's next Player Turn. If the model is a War Machine, the model is Shaken until the end of the owner's next Player Turn instead.
5+	**Malfunction** The shooting model loses a Health Point with no saves of any kind allowed.

Soft Cover (−1 to hit)

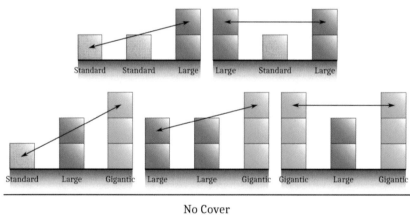

No Cover

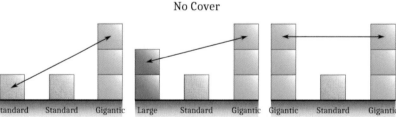

All other Height combinations yield either Hard Cover or no Line of Sight, depending on whether the target is completely obscured by the intervening model or not.

	Line of Sight	Cover
Fields	Covering (inside)	Soft Cover for non-Towering Presence
Forests	Covering (inside or behind)	Soft Cover
Hills	Opaque Terrain Covering (behind)	Soft Cover if partially on Hard Cover if entirely off
Impassable Terrain	Opaque Terrain	Hard Cover
Ruins	Covering (inside)	Hard Cover for non-Towering Presence
Walls	Covering (behind and Defending)	Hard Cover for non-Towering Presence

Melee Phase

Melee Phase Sequence

1	Start of the Melee Phase
2	Apply any No Longer Engaged
3	The Active Player chooses a combat that has not already been fought during this Melee Phase
4	Fight a Round of Combat
5	Repeat steps 2–4
6	Once all units that were Engaged in Combat at the start of the phase have fought, the Melee Phase ends

Combat Score Summary

Health Points Lost by Enemy Units	+1 for each Health Point
Overkill	+1 for each Health Point (maximum +3)
Charge	+1
Rank Bonus	+1 for each Full Rank after the first (maximum +3)
Standard	+1 for each Standard and Battle Standard Bearer
Flank Bonus	+1 or +2
Rear Bonus	+2 or +3

Round of Combat Sequence

1	Start of the Round of Combat
2	Choose a weapon
3	Make Way
4	Issue and accept Duels
5	Determine the Initiative Order
6	Roll Melee Attacks, starting with the first Initiative Step: 1. Allocate attacks 2. Roll to hit, to wound, saves, and remove casualties 3. Repeat 1. and 2. for the next Initiative Step
7	Calculate which side wins the Round of Combat. Losers roll Break Tests
8	Roll Panic Tests for units within 6″ of friendly Broken units
9	Decide to Restrain or to Pursue
10	Roll Flee Distances
11	Roll Pursuit Distances
12	Move Fleeing units
13	Move Pursuing units
14	Post-Combat Pivots and Post-Combat Reforms
15	Combat Reforms
16	End of the Round of Combat. Proceed to the next combat

Post-Game

Battle Points

Victory Point Difference		Battle Points	
Percentage of Army Points	(if playing with 4500 Army Points)	Winner	Loser
0–5%	0–225	10	10
>5–10%	226–450	11	9
>10–20%	451–900	12	8
>20–30%	901–1350	13	7
>30–40%	1351–1800	14	6
>40–50%	1801–2250	15	5
>50–70%	2251–3150	16	4
>70%	>3150	17	3
Winning Secondary Objective		+3	−3

Scoring Victory Points

Enemy unit	VP provided
Removed as a casualty	100% of point cost
Fleeing	50% of point cost
Shattered	50% of point cost
Shattered and Fleeing	100% of point cost
General or BSB removed as casualties	100% of point cost plus 200 VP each

Shattered: Units at 25% or less of their starting number of Health Points at the end of the game. Characters are counted separately from the units they have joined.

Attacks

Attack Sequence

1	Attacker allocates attacks if applicable.
2	Determine number of hits.
3	Attacker distributes hits if applicable.
4	Attacker rolls to wound; if successful, proceed.
5	Defender makes Armour Save rolls; if failed, proceed.
6	Defender makes Special Save rolls; if failed, proceed.
7	Defender removes Health Points or casualties.
8	Defender takes Panic Tests if necessary.

Close Combat To-Hit Table

Offensive Skill minus Defensive Skill	Needed roll to hit
4 or more	2+
1 to 3	3+
0 to −3	4+
−4 to −7	5+
−8 or less	6+

To-Wound Table

Strength minus Resilience	Needed roll to wound
2 or more	2+
1	3+
0	4+
−1	5+
−2 or less	6+

Armour Saves

Armour minus AP	Needed roll to disregard the wound
0 or less	No save possible
1	6+
2	5+
3	4+
4	3+
5 or 6	2+

Psychology

Panic Test Triggers

- A friendly unit is destroyed within 6″ of the unit (including Fleeing off the board).

- A friendly unit Breaks from Combat within 6″ of the unit.

- A friendly unit Flees through the unit's Unit Boundary.

- In a single phase, the unit suffers Health Point losses equal to or greater than 25% of the number of Health Points that it had at the start of the phase. This does not apply to single model units that started the game as a single model (i.e. with a starting number of 1 model on the Army List).

Units that fail a Panic Test Flee directly away from the closest enemy unit, or from the enemy unit which caused the Panic Test (Centre to Centre). Units do not take Panic Tests if they are Engaged in Combat, if they are already Fleeing, or if they already passed a Panic Test during this phase.

Shaken

A Shaken model cannot perform any of the following actions:

- Declare Charges
- Pursuit
- Overrun
- Advance Move
- March Move
- Reform (it can Combat Reform and Post-Combat Reform)
- Random Movement
- Shooting Attack

Fleeing

When a unit is Fleeing, it cannot perform any voluntary actions (a voluntary acti is an action that a unit would have the option to not perform). This includes (b is not limited to):

- Declare Charges
- Charge Reactions other than Flee
- Move in any way other than a Flee Move
- Shoot
- Channel
- Cast spells or activate One use only Special Items which need to be ac vated voluntarily

Models cannot receive Commanding Presence or Rally Around the Flag from Fleeing model.

Decimated

Units at 25% or less of their starting Health Points (the number taken from t Army List), including joined Characters, are referred to as Decimated. Decimat units must take their Rally Test at half their Discipline, rounding fractions up.

Probabilities

Chances to Pass a Discipline Test

Probabilities (in percentage) to pass a Discipline Test depending on the Discipline value of the unit (after modifiers) and the available rules:

Discipline	2	3	4	5	6	7	8	9	10
2D6	3	8	17	28	42	58	72	83	92
2D6 + reroll	5	16	31	48	66	83	92	97	99
2D6 + Minimised	7	20	36	52	68	81	89	95	98
2D6 + Minimised + reroll	14	36	59	77	90	96	99	99	99
2D6 + Maximised	1	2	5	11	19	32	48	64	80
2D6 + Maximised + reroll	1	4	10	20	35	54	73	87	96

Chances to Successfully Cast a Spell

Probabilities (in percentage) to successfully cast a spell depending on the Casting Value of the spell (after any modifiers to the casting roll) and on the number of Mag Dice:

Casting Value	3+	4+	5+	6+	7+	8+	9+	10+	11+	12+	13+	14+	15+	16+	17+	18+	Miscast
1D6	67	50	33	17	0	0	0	0	0	0	0	0	0	0	0	0	0
2D6	97	92	83	72	58	42	28	17	8	3	0	0	0	0	0	0	0
3D6	99	99	98	95	91	84	74	63	50	38	26	16	10	5	2	1	3
4D6	98	98	98	98	98	97	94	90	84	76	66	56	44	34	24	16	10
5D6	100	100	100	99	99	99	99	98	97	94	90	85	78	70	60	50	21

24   About this publication

24.A   Publishers Note

The 9th Age as a game has engaged and fascinated me many hours in the past and so it will in the future. I strongly believe an easy and cheap access to a well-printed and bound rulebook will ease joining and enjoying this gorgeous game to any interested people. The current publication has been created for the simple reason of supporting the grand game which – in my opinion – The 9th Age is. There is no intention on the publisher's side to generate any profit by providing this print work. Pricing is calculated to gain less than one Euro margin while any margin earned by sales of the actual document will be donated to The 9th Age project after having covered the costs related to this publication.

This print is the closest possible version to the online publication of the rulebook. Neither rules nor references have been changed. Any changes done compared with the original formatting were required due to the transformation into the US letter format, others result from requirements of publishing and printing. Changes to the original content comprise only the addition of this chapter, the imprint and one minor change in Summaries.   - Kevin

24.B   9th Age Licensing

https://www.the-ninth-age.com/index.php?terms/#term583

The 9th Age ("T9A") is a non-profit association that does not engage in commercial for-profit activities. All of T9A documents, which include: T9A Basic Rule Book, T9A Paths of Magic Book and/or any of the individual T9A Army Books (collectively "T9A Materials") are provided free of charge.

1. Definitions

sketch or three-dimensional work relative to geography, topography, architecture or science; a performance; a broadcast; a compilation of data to the extent it is protected as a copyrightable work.

- "You" means an individual or entity exercising rights under this License who has not previously violated the terms of this License with respect to the Work, or who has received express permission from the Licensor to exercise rights under this License despite a previous violation.
- "Reproduce" means to make copies of the Work by any means including without limitation by sound or visual recordings and the right of fixation and reproducing fixations of the Work, including storage of a protected performance or phonogram in digital form or other electronic medium.

2. Fair Dealing Rights Nothing in this License is intended to reduce, limit, or restrict any uses free from copyright or rights arising from limitations or exceptions that are provided for in connection with the copyright protection under copyright law or other applicable laws.

3. License Grant Subject to the terms and conditions of this License, Licensor hereby grants You a personal worldwide, royalty-free, non-exclusive, perpetual (for the duration of the applicable copyright) license to exercise the rights in the Work as stated below:

- to Reproduce the Work, to incorporate the Work into one or more Collections, and to Reproduce the Work as incorporated in the Collections for personal use;
- to create and Reproduce Adaptations for personal use provided that any such Adaptation, including any translation in any medium, takes reasonable steps to clearly label, demarcate or otherwise identify that changes were made to the original Work. For example, a translation could be marked "The original work was translated from English to Spanish," or a modification could indicate "The original work has been modified.";
- to make commercial use of the Work so long as you agree that you shall: DEFEND, INDEMNIFY AND HOLD HARMLESS T9A and any of its related parties from and against any and all third party claims and liabilities (including, without limitation, REASONABLE ATTORNEYS' FEES AND COSTS), regardless of the form of action, arising out of or in connection with a claim that the Work infringes, violates or misappropriates a valid third party copyright or other proprietary right. Additions to the work may be provided in a digital document or in printed format (such as a book) either at the beginning of the document or may be added on at the end of the document. No modifications to the Work are permitted for commercial distribution without the express permission of the Licensor.

4. Restrictions The license granted in Section 3 above is expressly made subject to and limited by the following restrictions:

- You may Distribute the Work only under the terms of this License. You must include a copy of, or the Uniform Resource Identifier (URI) for, this License with every copy of the Work You Distribute. You may not offer or impose any terms on the Work that restrict the terms of this License or the ability of the recipient of the Work to exercise the rights granted to that recipient under the terms of the License. You may not sublicense the Work. You must keep intact all notices that refer to this License and to the disclaimer of warranties with every copy of the Work You Distribute. When You Distribute the Work, You may not impose any effective technological measures on the Work that restrict the ability of a recipient of the Work from You to exercise the rights granted to that recipient under the terms of the License. This Section 4(a) applies to the Work as incorporated in a Collection, but this does not require the Collection apart from the Work itself to be made subject to the terms of this License.
- If You Distribute the Work or any Adaptations or Collections, You must, unless a request has been made pursuant to Section 4(a), keep intact all copyright notices for the Work and provide, reasonable to the medium or means You are utilizing: (i) the name of the Original Author (or pseudonym, if applicable) if supplied, and/or if the Original Author and/or Licensor designate another party or parties (e.g., a sponsor institute, publishing entity, journal) for attribution ("Attribution Parties") in Licensor's copyright notice, terms of service or by other reasonable means, the name of such party or parties; (ii) the title of the Work if supplied; (iii) to the extent reasonably practicable, the URI, if any, that Licensor specifies to be associated with the Work, unless such URI does not refer to the copyright notice or licensing information for the Work; and, (iv) consistent with Section 3(b), in the case of an Adaptation, a credit identifying the use of the Work in the Adaptation (e.g., "French translation of the Work by Original Author," or "Screenplay based on original Work by Original Author").
- Non-waivable Compulsory License Schemes. In those jurisdictions in which the right to collect royalties through any statutory or compulsory licensing scheme cannot be waived, the Licensor reserves the exclusive right to collect such royalties for any exercise by You of the rights granted under this License;
- Waivable Compulsory License Schemes. In those jurisdictions in which the right to collect royalties through any statutory or compulsory licensing scheme can be waived, the Licensor reserves the exclusive right to collect such royalties for any exercise by You of the rights granted under this License if Your exercise of such rights is for a purpose or use which is otherwise than noncommercial as permitted under Section 4(b) and otherwise waives the right to collect royalties through any statutory or compulsory licensing scheme; and,

- Voluntary License Schemes. The Licensor reserves the right to collect royalties, whether individually or, in the event that the Licensor is a member of a collecting society that administers voluntary licensing schemes, via that society, from any exercise by You of the rights granted under this License that is for a purpose or use which is otherwise than noncommercial as permitted under Section 4(c).
- Except as otherwise agreed in writing by the Licensor or as may be otherwise permitted by applicable law, if You Reproduce or Distribute the Work either by itself or as part of any Adaptations or Collections, You must not distort, mutilate, modify or take other derogatory action in relation to the Work which would be prejudicial to the Original Author's honor or reputation. Licensor agrees that in those jurisdictions (e.g. Japan), in which any exercise of the right granted in Section 3(b) of this License (the right to make Adaptations) would be deemed to be a distortion, mutilation, modification or other derogatory action prejudicial to the Original Author's honor and reputation, the Licensor will waive or not assert, as appropriate, this Section, to the fullest extent permitted by the applicable national law, to enable You to reasonably exercise Your right under Section 3(b) of this License (right to make Adaptations) but not otherwise.

5. Representations, Warranties and Disclamer UNLESS OTHERWISE MUTUALLY AGREED TO BY THE PARTIES IN WRITING, LICENSOR OFFERS THE WORK AS-IS AND MAKES NO REPRESENTATIONS OR WARRANTIES OF ANY KIND CONCERNING THE WORK, EXPRESS, IMPLIED, STATUTORY OR OTHERWISE, INCLUDING, WITHOUT LIMITATION, WARRANTIES OF TITLE, MERCHANTIBILITY, FITNESS FOR A PARTICULAR PURPOSE, NONINFRINGEMENT, OR THE ABSENCE OF LATENT OR OTHER DEFECTS, ACCURACY, OR THE PRESENCE OF ABSENCE OF ERRORS, WHETHER OR NOT DISCOVERABLE. SOME JURISDICTIONS DO NOT ALLOW THE EXCLUSION OF IMPLIED WARRANTIES, SO SUCH EXCLUSION MAY NOT APPLY TO YOU.

6. Limitation on Liability EXCEPT TO THE EXTENT REQUIRED BY APPLICABLE LAW, IN NO EVENT WILL LICENSOR BE LIABLE TO YOU ON ANY LEGAL THEORY FOR ANY SPECIAL, INCIDENTAL, CONSEQUENTIAL, PUNITIVE OR EXEMPLARY DAMAGES ARISING OUT OF THIS LICENSE OR THE USE OF THE WORK, EVEN IF LICENSOR HAS BEEN ADVISED OF THE POSSIBILITY OF SUCH DAMAGES.

7. Termination This License and the rights granted hereunder will terminate automatically upon any breach by You of the terms of this License. Individuals or entities who have received Adaptations or Collections from You under this License, however, will not have their licenses terminated provided such individuals or entities remain in full compliance with those licenses. Sections 1, 2, 5, 6, 7, and 8 will survive any termination of this License. Subject to the above terms and conditions, the license granted here is perpetual (for the duration of the applicable copyright in the Work). Notwithstanding the above, Licensor reserves the right to release the Work under different license terms or to stop distributing the Work at any time; provided, however that any such election will not serve to withdraw this License (or any other license that has been, or is required to be, granted under the terms of this License), and this License will continue in full force and effect unless terminated as stated above.

8. Miscellaneous

- Each time You Distribute the Work or a Collection, the Licensor offers to the recipient a license to the Work on the same terms and conditions as the license granted to You under this License.
- Each time You Distribute an Adaptation, Licensor offers to the recipient a license to the original Work on the same terms and conditions as the license granted to You under this License.
- If any provision of this License is invalid or unenforceable under applicable law, it shall not affect the validity or enforceability of the remainder of the terms of this License, and without further action by the parties to this agreement, such provision shall be reformed to the minimum extent necessary to make such provision valid and enforceable.
- No term or provision of this License shall be deemed waived and no breach consented to unless such waiver or consent shall be in writing and signed by the party to be charged with such waiver or consent.
- This License constitutes the entire agreement between the parties with respect to the Work licensed here. There are no understandings, agreements or representations with respect to the Work not specified here. Licensor shall not be bound by any additional provisions that may appear in any communication from You. This License may not be modified without the mutual written agreement of the Licensor and You.
- The rights granted under, and the subject matter referenced, in this License were drafted utilizing the terminology of the Berne Convention for the Protection of Literary and Artistic Works (as amended on September 28, 1979), the Rome Convention of 1961, the WIPO Copyright Treaty of 1996, the WIPO Performances and Phonograms Treaty of 1996 and the Universal Copyright Convention (as revised on July 24, 1971). These rights and subject matter take effect in the relevant jurisdiction in which the License terms are sought to be enforced according to the corresponding provisions of the implementation of those treaty provisions in the applicable national law. If the standard suite of rights granted under applicable copyright law includes additional rights not granted under this License, such additional rights are deemed to be included in the License; this License is not intended to restrict the license of any rights under applicable law.

25 Alphabetical Index

A | B | C | D | E | F | G | H | I | K | L | M | N | O | P | Q | R | S | T | U | V | W

12326110R10079

Made in the USA
Monee, IL
24 September 2019